T0208302

Dr. Touhami Negra

# Kairwan through the Ages

iUniverse, Inc.
Bloomington

iUniverse books may be ordered through booksellers or by contacting:

iUniverse
1663 Liberty Drive
Bloomington, IN 47403
www.iuniverse.com
1-800-Authors (1-800-288-4677)

Because of the dynamic nature of the Internet, any web addresses or links contained in this book may have changed since publication and may no longer be valid. The views expressed in this work are solely those of the author and do not necessarily reflect the views of the publisher, and the publisher hereby disclaims any responsibility for them.

Any people depicted in stock imagery provided by Thinkstock are models, and such images are being used for illustrative purposes only.

Certain stock imagery © Thinkstock.

ISBN: 978-1-4502-9160-6 (sc)
ISBN: 978-1-4502-9161-3 (ebook)

Printed in the United States of America

iUniverse rev. date: 03/17/2011

# The writer's biography
## (born, 1928, died 1997)

The late Dr. Touhami Negra, God bless his soul, was first and foremost my brother and the eldest brother in the Negra's household, and I am the youngest. I consider Dr. Touhami, not only a brother, but a father because he used to be a great help to me and to my siblings in our education, his caring about our jobs, our promotion in our posts and our standard of living. Whenever there was a problem concerning me or the family, he was there to help or to solve it. Besides the great role that he played in the family, he had social eminence and prestige. He was venerated by the people of Kairwan, both the rich and the poor for his high morals, his generosity and lavishness with the needy and his moral support for those who asked for his help.

Dr. Touhami was first educated in the "Kuttab" (Koranic school) and "Madrassa" (primary school) in Kairwan. At the age of eleven, he learned heart and soul the 60 parts of the Holy Koran. When he was 13, he completed his primary studies in Kairwan and moved to Tunis to pursue his secondary and high education in theology in the Zeitouna Mosque. He obtained "Attahssil" (the Baccalaureat, G.C.E.) at the age of 19, and "Al Allimia" (the B.A.) at the age of 22. He was appointed a teacher of theology, then a principal in a Zeitouna secondary school branch in a small town in the center west of Tunisia called Feriana; Three years later, he was appointed in Okhba Mosque in Kairwan as a secondary school teacher in the same major. Two years after Tunisia had its independence, exactlty in

1958, the government built a secondary school in Kairwan with modern standards of education, so the students and teachers moved from Okhba Mosque to that school which bore the name of "Lycee de Jeunes Filles" (Secondary girls'school). My brother taught in it for four years until 1962. I remember I was one of his students in 1960, 1961.

In the meantime, Dr. Touhami showed a great interest in politics and in the national problems of the country. In 1962, he adhered to the unique political party at that time, "The Constitutional Tunisian Party" (Al Hizb Addestouri Attounissi) under the leadership of president Habib Bourguiba, the first president of Tunisia. In 1963, he was elected member of parliament at the age of 33. He was the representative of the governorate of his native town, Kairwan. His first term which lasted five years allowed him to acquire a political experience and to visit many brotherly and friendly countries, like The Soviet Union, Lebanon, Palestine Syria, in addition to some western and eastern European countries.

In 1964, he left Kairwan and moved to Tunis. In 1966, he was nominated general secretary of "the College of Islamic Studies and Islamic Jurisprudence", and that nomination made him return to what is scholastic and academic. He started writing a Ph. thesis on the following topic: "The Psychology of the Story in the Holy Koran." He obtained his doctorate in 1973 from Algiers University. His thesis was published in 1974. This thesis was an incentive for him to become a writer of religious subjects. From 1974 until the early 1990s, he wrote four books on the following religious topics:

1. "In the light of the Koran and the Sunna"

2. " The belief of Resurrection in Islam

3. "The Sunnits' and the Mootazillas'(a religious sect) approach as to the interpretation of the Koran"

4. "Fields of Research in the Holy Koran and its various interpretations"

Besides his writing theological thesis and treatises, Dr. Touhami wrote in 1960, 1961 teaching books in Arabic grammar and morphology for secondary school student. In 1963, he wrote his history book, "Kairwan through the Ages".

This great interest in writing altogether with his dynamic political activities made president Zine Al Abidin Ben Ali, the existing president, give him high-ranked positions in government and universities. In 1987, he was appointed respectively Chancellor of Zeitouna Islamic University and president emeritus of the High Islamic Council.

Dr. Touhami's fame as a Tunisian scholar spread all over the Arab, Moslem and Western worlds. He was invited to take part in many world conferences and seminars in Saudi Arabia, Morocco, Lebanon, Spain and France, seminars about the reconciliation between the three heavenly religions, Islam, Christianity and Judaism, and other seminars and symposia.

He also wrote religious articles in many Gulf and Arab magazines. When I was teaching in Riyadh, Saudi Arabia (1996,2006), I came into contact with the staff of "king Faisal Islamic Center (Al Faisalia), I was submitted the collection of the lectures that my brother had given and the articles that he had written which numbered to100 and amounted to 800 pages. I would have liked to compile them into a book and have them published, but they are still waiting.

Dr. Touhami was assigned a Tunisian TV programme between 1975 and 1980 entitled "Religion and Life". It appealed both to the intellectuals and the laymen; it gained such a great popularity in Tunisia and in some Arab neighboring countries like Algeria and Libya. I remember that whenever I went for a walk around Kairwan, people stopped me just to express their pleasure and delight for the programme and asked me to give their best regards to my brother Touhami who was then living in Tunis.

In the late eightees, Dr. Touhami was assigned to give lectures by the Saudi government in the "Arab Center for Security Studies" in Riyadh. The topics were about "Islam and Security." Those lectures lasted until 1991. In 1992, he was nominated Professor Emeritus in "Al Ain University" in the United Arab Emirates to give lectures on theological studies and at the same time inspect the technical colleges in the U.A.E. teaching religious subjects. He worked in the Emirates until 1995.

He returned to Tunisia in July 1995 and kept to bed because he befell ill. He suffered from an incurable heart disease until he passed away on September 23, 1997.

Dr. Touhami died physically, but he did not die spiritually because the invaluable legacy that he left immortalized him and let scholars and laymen remember him through his publications. In commemoration of his memory, the Tunisian government gave his name to some streets both in Kairwan and in Tunis.

Will the name of Dr. Touhami Negra shine for ever over Islamic institutes east and west, and will God Almighty bestow on his pure soul His mercy and His bountiful rewards in this life and in the life-to come.

# Preface

This book is a modest translation of "Kairwan through The Ages". Although I did not translate the whole book and skipped some parts which seemed to me minutely detailed, in addition to my paraphrasing most of the poems in the original book, I think the translation I made is comprehensive and includes the main ideas dealt with in the translated book.

The book can be divided into five main parts. The first part deals with the Islamic conquest of Ifrikya by some eminent Arabs from Medina and Mecca. The second part is called 'The Era of Governors'. It was the time when Ifrikya began to develop at all levels and Kairwan was made its capital. In the third part Kairwan was shown in the peak of development and urbanization under the Aghlabites'reign. The fourth part brings out the gradual decline of Kairwan and its causes during the last period of the Aghlabites' declining reign and the rising of the Ubaidis whose reign did not last more than 65 years. The fifth part highlights the reign of the Sanhajis, a Berber tribe who took over the rule from the Arabs. It was the period which witnesses the deadly conflicts between the Sunnits and the Shi'its, the disastrous fall of Kairwan and the removal of the Fatimids, a Shi'it ruling dynasty from Kairwan to Mahdia, then to Cairo in Egypt.

Let me now develop this outline into a synopsis summarizing the main events that took place after the Islamic conquest of Ifrikya and the causes that led to the calamitous fall of Ifrikya in general and Kairwan, its capital, in particular after six centuries of full thriving and prosperity.

It is in the first century of the Hegira in the year 50, which corresponds to the sixth century ( ) that a Moslem army under the leadership of Okhba Ben Nafaa from Medina conquered Ifrikya (Tunisia) after an authoritative command of Othman Ibnu Affan, the Commander of the Faithful and one of Prophet Mohamed's companion. When Okhba and his army arrived in Ifrikya, they looked for a secure place where to alight; they found in Kairwan, an inland area in the center of Ifrikya, a convenient settlement and a safe garrison for their soldiers and their animals.

Just a few years after a victorious battle against the Romans, Kairwan developed so rapidly during the era of governors that it became the capital of Ifrikya. It knew during that period such an unparalleled religious, political and economical development that it started to shine over Ifrikya and the neighboring countries surrounding it, Libya, Algeria and Morocco.

With the advent of the Aghlabites, a tribe from the Arab peninsula, Kairwan knew an unprecedent boom during their reign. The Aghlabites' reign was not only in Ifrikya, but it extended to other countries like Libya, Algeria, Morocco and some south Mediterrean European towns like Sicily in Italy, Andalusia in Spain, Malta and Cyprus with Kairwan as the mother town and the capital. Kairwan reached the peak of civilization and development during the Aghlabites'era which lasted more two hundred years. Kairwan ranked third after Medina in the Arabian peninsula and Baghdad in Irak. It had a very prosperous industry, agriculture and economy, along with a developed religious, educational and cultural activity. However, this this felicitous situation did not last because the last Aghlabites' princes misruled their principalities and indulged in the money of the government and the people to gratify their wishes in such a way that their decline entailed the decline of Kairwan. Finally, they lost their power and the rule of Kairwan and Ifrikya passed on to another dynasty, the Ubaidis.

The Ubaidi era did not last but 65 years, and this is because of the continuous mutinies and uprisings that shook Ifrikya in general and

Kairwan in particular and led to their weakening and accordingly to their gradual fall. In fact, during the Ubaidis'reign, many violent and sometimes bloody wars took place between the two Moslem sects, the Sunnits and the Shi'its. The conflicts intensified, especially in Kairwan, so much so that they ended up with the removal of the government from Kairwan to Mahdia, in the south east, then to Cairo in Egypt.

Kairwan began to lose its political, economical and cultural power. Nevertheless, it remained the religious capital of Ifrikya and a referential authority for the Sunnits along with their ideology.

When the ubaidi princes were vanquished and fled to Egypt, the Sanhajis, a Berber dynasty took over. The Tunisian historian, Ibnu Khaldun wrote that with the coming of the Berbers into power, Arab civilization and prestige disappeared from Ifrikya. When the Fatimid princes left Kairwan and transferred the rule from Mahdia first, then to Egypt, thet entrusted the government of Ifrikya to the Sanhaji. Unfortunately, the Sanhaji were incompetent rulers. They let the conflicts intensify between the Shi'its and Sunnits. When they sided with the Sunnits and let down the Shi'its, the Fatimid rulers who were Shi'its sent in retalation to Ifrikya a tribe of unruly nomads from Upper Egypt, called the Hilalis, who devastated most of Ifriya's towns destroying everything on their way and making havoc all over the country and especially in Kairwan.

Kairwan was wholly destroyed; its mosques, institutes, market places and ramparts. The 'House of Wisdom' (Beitul Hikma) which stood for the high intellectual level that Kairwan had enjoyed since the Aghlabites' was transferred to Cairo along with its rich collection of books. Most of Kairwan's scholars left for Cairo, Andalusia and Sicily. The religious and intellectual circles that Kairwan's mosques delighted in its heydays disappeared. By and large, Kairwan plunged in deep darkness. Besides, it suffered from such an incurable economic crisis that, unlike Tunis, it became unable to rise again.

Kairwan's wretched condition saddened its writers and poets so dismally that they wrote eligies bemoaning the calamitous fall of Kairwan.

It took almost seven centuries for Kairwan to experience a glimpse of revival. As a matter of fact, it was just after independence that the first president of Tunisia, Habib Bourguiba, restored Kairwan's glorious past by renovating some of its ruined ramparts, mosques, mosoleums and institutes. He restored the prestigious past of Rakkada by building a palace there, and by restoring the detrimental Aghlabites'pools. He comemorated the olden days of Kairwan during religious feasts like the 'Muled' (TheProphet's birthday).

The interest in Kairwan increased with the existing president Zine Al Abidin Ben Ali. Ben Ali is reviving Kairwan's glorious Islamic civilization by asking the regional and the national authorities to hold continuous forums and seminars on Kairwan's Islamic history and civilization, and by encouraging historians to write about its prestigious past. Besides, he ordered that Kairwan should be honored by calling the year 2009, (1430) the year of "Kairwan, the Capital of Islamic Culture" in recognition of this town's prestigious past.

*This is president Bourguiba, the first president of Tunisia during his visit to Kairwan in the year 1959. He is delivering a speech on the pulpit of Okhba Bin Nafaa Mosque on the occasion of Mulled (the Prophet's birthday)*

"I can imagine how in this ancient and venerable city, Kairwan, the deep thoughts and varied sciences spread out throughout Ifrikya and the Arab Maghreb. It is from this prestigiously religious temple (the Big Mosque) that came forth the outstanding religious sciences and wise legislation which served as the foundations of Islamic civilization and philosophy in North Africa."

This is a synopsis of the speech delivered by Habib Bourguiba, on the pulpit of the Big Mosque in Kairwan on the occasion of the Mouled (birthday) of the Prophet Mohamed (PUB) on December 14th. 1959, which corresponds to 11th. Of Rabii Al Awal, 1379.

# An introduction to
# "Kairwan through the Ages": Othman Al Kaaek

Othman Al Kaaek is a contemporary Tunisian historian who lived in the early 20thc.and died in the last decade or so of the same century. He became famous in the mid- twentieth century as a historian, archeologist and professor of Tunisian history in Tunis University. He was versed in all the historical periods of Tunisian history from the times of the Phoenicians, the Carthagenians, the Berbers, the Romans, the Moslems, the Turkish dominion and the French colonization until the time Tunisia won its independence in the 1950s.

Othman Kaeek read Dr. Touhami Negra's book, "Kairwan through the Ages" and wrote this introduction.This is a concise synopsis of what he wrote:

"I welcomed heartily this valuable book when it was offered to me by professor Touhami Negra. I was actually lucky to be the first to read it as a manuscript before it was published. I found it richly informative, clearly expressive and easy to read both by the learned man and the layman. It was written in a fluent and coherent style. It came into being after deep researches made by its meritorious and judiciuos writer. I found it very interesting and exciting to read especially that it dealt with an important part of history, the Islamic history of Tunisia in general and the history of Kairwan in particular.

It goes without saying that Kairwan deserved to be called the very Capital of Ifrikya and the Maghreb in the period between the first century of the Hegir to the the 6ᵗʰ c. of the same date, that is, between the Gregorian 7thc. to the 13thc. Kairwan was undoubtedly the mother and the honor of Islam in North Africa and some southern parts of the Mediteranean as was written on one of its seven-city gates.

Kairwan embraced a blend of several civilizations. First, European from Greek, Roman, Byzantine and Andalusian. Second, Tunisia was originally Berber and then Arab. An assortment of the most important manuscripts of the Phoenicians, the Berbers and the Romans were translated into Arabic during the heyday of Arab civilization. It was also in Kairwan that academic studies were given in Arabic, Berber and Hebrew. It was in mosques and prestigious institutes that lectures were given on the interpretations of the Holy Koran, Hadith (the Prophet's tradition and utterances), jurisprudence and sophism. There were recitations of the Koran, and comparative studies of doctrines and idologies were made like the comparison between the Sunna and the Shiaa doctrines. It was also in those institutes that sciences like Maths, Physics, Chemistry, Medicine and Astrology were taught.

Kairwan cared for the scientific development of agriculture, industry, trade with the Saharian regions and also the sea-coast trade, especially with the Romans and the people of Northen Europe.

Kairwan was a meeting place of art , poetry and literature. Its art was the quintessence of Greek, Persian, Byzantine and Berber arts. Its architecture was a fusion of various eastern architectures and at the same time the starting point of a new architecture unknown in Ifrikya before the Islamic conquest. For example, the architectural design of Okhba Bin Nafaa's Mosque was emulated by many mosques in the Arab world. This is the case of Ibnu Touloun Mosque in Cairo, the Omayyad Mosque in Kordoba and the Mosque in Palermo, Italy. Not only did mosques emulate Okhba Mosque architecture, but also some churches in Italy, Spain, France and Mexico were influenced by this architecture.

By and large, Kairwan was at that time the Capital city of civilization, east and west. It was radiant with its science, art , literature and architecture.

So whatever valuable writing or research is done on the Islamic history of Kairwan is heartily welcome. This is the case of professorTouhami Negra's book, "Kairwan through the Ages" which I read with great excitement and pleasure. As a matter of fact, what was written on Kairwan before was a great deal, but what reached us was almost so insignificant that one wonders what happened to the thousands of books written in the Aghlabites'era, the Fatimides', like the books of Al Khadhi Annoumaan, the books of the physician Ibnul Jazzar, the books issued in the Sanhaji era, such as the book by Ibnul Arab, Al Shirazi, Attabari, Ibnu Saadoun, Ibnu Rashik, Ibnu Sharaf and many others.

Not only the books were the landmarks of Kairwan's flourishing civilization, but also its buildings, its palaces, its market places, its industry; all these rich landmarks had disappeared,too. What happened to the city of Kairwan and to the towns in its outskirts, like Sabra, Al Abassia, Rakkada and Al Mansouria; they disappeared in their turn, and only a few ruins were left as if this great civilization had not existed at all. Was not the coming out of these few books like "Kairwan through the Ages" an opportunity to vivify the prestigious history of this town? Kairwan would have plunged into a state of complete oblivion, had not her sons done their utmost to revive her history. We can enjoy nowadays the sweet remembrances of Kairwan's heydays, its illustrious scholars, poets, scientific men who had left their footprints on the European civilization. We are actually grateful for the endeavor made by the modern intellectual elite of Kairwan, like Touhami Negra whose valuable work will remain an everlasting message for this generation and the generations to come to discover what they do not know on the flourishing Islamic civilization and Islam in the North African continent, and particularly in Kairwan.

# The Conquest Of Ifrikya

Muswar Ibn Mahrama said: "I left my home one night and made for the Mosque (the Prophet's Mosque in Medina). There was Uthman Ibin Affaan performing his prayer just where the Prophet (PUB) used to pray. I stood and prayed behind him. Then, after the prayer, he sat down and started his long invocations of God until the muezzin called for the Ishaa prayer. Then, he set off back home. I stood up and greeted him. He looked at me and said: "Hello Ibnou Mahrama. I asked God's guidance as to my sending an army for the conquest of Ifrikya. What do you think?" I said: "Would God Almighty guide the Commander of the Faithful along the right path. That Ifrikya will be conquered as you ordered." I answered. "Would you call the followers of the Prophet (PUB) for a meeting so that I will consult with them lengthily and have their opinion." He added. Uthman invited them in his speech to volunteer for the conquest of Ifrikya.

Then on the 27tth. Of the Hegira Year, an army of 20 thousand followers and friends of the Prophet (PUB) under the command of Abdullah Sarrah left Makkah and trekked through the wilderness of Barka and Tripoli in Libya until they reached Ifrikya (Tunisia).They alighted not far from the town of Sbeitla in the south west, which was then the settlement of the army of the Roman king Jerjir. When the latter learned about the arrival of that army from the Arabian Peninsula, he went for their assault with a huge army of one hundred thousand Roman and Berber soldiers. When the two armies met, they went into a fierce battle which ended up with the death of Jirjir and the massacre and dispersal of his army. Finally, they gave in and signed a peace treaty.

It was then that the commander of the Muslim army sent a messenger to the khalif Uthman Ibn Affaan in Medina to herald the good tidings of God's granting the Muslim army a great victory over the Romans in Ifrikya .The messenger was Abdullah Ibn Zubair. When Abdullah reached the Medina, he heralded the good tidings to the khalif. The latter asked him to make public the great victory in the Mosque. Ibnou Zubair stood up in the pulpit and spoke to the people. First, he thanked and praised God, and then he said: "O people, we made for the destination that you knew about already, and we were in company of a leader who was answerable to the Commander of the Faithful's testament. He led us, soldiers, towards the designed destination. We alighted at noon and had a rest at night. However, we decamped hastily from the arid lands and settled for long in the fertile lands. God Almighty had bestowed on us quietude and serenity until we reached Ifrikya. When we alighted there, we could hear nothing but the neighing of horses, the grumbling of camels and the resounding of weapons. We settled down for a few days to heal our bruises and to ease our pains. Then a messenger was sent to the enemy camp to ask them to convert to Islam, but they refused. Then we asked them to pay a tribute as a sign of their submission, but their refusal was absolute. So, we took legal action against them. Nevertheless, we continued to send them messengers for thirteen consecutive nights. When we despaired of any reconciliation, our leader stood up and spoke to us stating first the favor that Jihad (holy war) had on he who was armed with patience and faith, and who sacrificed himself for God's cause.

After delivering this long speech, we set out for the encounter of our enemies whom we killed so ruthlessly that the day ended up with thousands of casualties on both sides. Many of our soldiers were martyrized on that day for the cause of Islam.

Then our warriors and theirs spent the night peacefully. We Muslims spent the whole night reciting the Koran, and nothing could be heard but the chanters whose reciting sounded like the buzzing of bees. As for the infidels, they spent the night drinking and gambling. Early in the morning, we lined up and marched against our enemy making a fierce assault on them. God the Merciful filled us with patience and bestowed on us His victory so that by the end of that day, Ifrikya was conquered. We seized a lot of booty and took hold of large lands.

After the conquest, Abdullah Ibn Abi Sarh returned to Egypt after having spent one year and two months in Ifrikya. This conquest was known under the name of the Obeidullah's conquest because seven of the Prophet's companions who bore the names of Abdullah took part in that conquest.

When Muaouia Ibn Abi Sofian was appointed Commander of the Faithful, he sent another army for the conquest of Ifrikya under the leadership of Muaiouia Ibn Hadij Al Kendi in the Hegira year 45 and conquered Sussa, Bizerta and Jelloula. Then he sent a navy force to Sicily and invaded it,too. Finally, he returned to Egypt. So Muaouia Ibn Abi Sufain had to appoint another governor to Ifrikya. It was Okhba Bin Naffaa El Fehri. The historian, Abu Al Arab, stated that "Muaouia Ibn Hadij conquered Ifrikya three times cosecutively in the hegira years, 34, 45 and 50.

*The entrance of Abi Zammaa Al Balaoui Mosque. This pious man
who came from Medina was the Prophet's fellow and Barber.
He took part in a holy war against the infidels, died in Jeloula, a
town in the outskirts of Kairwan, and was buried in Kairwan.
His tomb was inside this mosque, which bears his name.*

## I. The mapping out of Kairwan

When Ibn Hadij returned to Egypt, the people of Ifrikya rebelled against the laws he had set up after being obedient and submissive for some time. So Mouaouia sent them an army of ten thousand soldiers under the command of Okhba Ibn Naffaa El fehri. The latter conquered many of the Roman forts while on his way until he reached Kairwan where a Roman fortress going under the name of "Khamounia" was installed. He consulted with the commanders of his army and said to them: "You

Arab companions, I think that you have to conquer a city in this area and make it into a military encampment." His companions complied with his request, and some of them suggested that if the city is near the sea, that means that it should be implemented with a garrison for the defense of its people from the enemy. Okhba answered that he feared it would be invaded by the king of Constantinople and suggested that it should be quite a good distance away from the sea so that the sea pirates would not reach it and devastate it. He wanted the army to be installed close to the marsh. But his companions claimed that its being close to the marsh might cause their death since its winter would be bitterly cold and its summer overwhelmingly hot. He added that the marsh was the most convenient settlement because most of their animals were camels. Besides, he reminded them that the Berbers were converted to Christianity, and once they came to the end of the invasion, they would be so exhausted that they would not be able to fight any more. Thus their encampment close to the marsh would make their animals safe from the attacks both of the Berbers and the Romans. Finally and after long debates, they reached a consensus. It was in Kairwan that they settled.

The first buildings to be installed there were the mosque and the principality or prince's residence. Then people began to build their houses so that the area became populated within a short time. Furthermore, stables for animals were built everywhere in the town.

The Arab historian, Ibn Khaldoun, pointed out that the Arabs as a rule did not take into account what is best when they mapped out their city. He gave the example of three renouned cities at that time, Kufa, Basra and Kairwan, showing how the Arab architects, cared only about the safety of their animals when they built their cities close to nomadic and arid pathways in such a way that the position and location of their cities were far from what really urban cities should be positioned, that is in fertile areas which are undoubtedly quite convenient for human habitation. As a result, once those cities were assaulted by the enemy, they were easily devastated and wiped out.

Actually, the Arabs did not give as much importance to the safety of their animals as they gave to the appropriate military position of their cities which should be, according to their conception, distant from the perils of the sea and the sudden and surprising assault of the Roman fleet.

The rulers who governed Ifrikya and those who came after them settled for centuries there, that is quite distant from the sea, and none had the idea of moving quite near it except for political reasons, so that Ifrikya became the cradle of civilization and urbanization in spite of building its big cities far from the sea.

Ibn Khaldoun described Kairwan when he visited it in the 4th.C of the Hegira year as "the greatest city in the Maghreb with its huge and numberless trades, its tremendous wealth and the beauty of its architectural buildings and market-places.

Bekir, another historian, wrote that Kairwan used to have fourteen gates to its ramparts. Its market-place stretched along a road beginning from the mosque in the north and ending up at Rabii's gate southward. The road which was about two miles long was lined up with shops and workshops. It was Hisham Ibn Abdel Malik, the king at that time, who ordered that the market place should be arrayed as such. Dr. Ahmed Fekhri, a contemporary Egyptian historian, pointed out that the city of Kairwan has preserved its beauty and order since that time.

It was said that when Abu Abdullah Al Mahdi took over the reign from the Aghlabites and penetrated Kairwan, he was fascinated by its vivacity and its flourishing development which was an evidence of its prestigious civilization.

What is known about the Romans is that they always settled down in fertile and inhabited areas with a lot of grass and water. When the Muslim conquerors seized Kairwan and made it the capital of the Maghreb, it became prosperous and its inhabitants became well off. Its ramparts which were rebuilt by the Aghlabite prince, Moez Ibn Badis at the end of the 4$^{th}$C. had a sphere of about 12 miles. Besides, all the small towns surrounding it like Rakkada, Jellula, Sabra, and Al Abassia were populated and full of business.

*Okhba Mosque is the oldest vestige in the Arab Maghreb. It was erected by Okhba Bin Nafaa just after the conquest of Ifrikya*

## II.Kairwan, the capital of Ifrikya

Since the foundation of Ifrikya in 50 of the Hegira year until the installment of the Aghlabites'government in 184, Ifrikya had been under the authority of governors who ruled under the command of the Ummayads, then the Abbasside khalifates. The governor lived in the emirate's house. His duty consisted of presiding over the city council, the treasury, the mail and many other duties. He had also to appoint civil servants for the management of the various counties in the country. There were at that time five main counties in Ifrikya: Tunis, Constantine in Algeria, the Djerid area in the south of Tunisia, Tripoli in Libya and the Maghreb in Morocco.

Thirty successive governors had ruled over Ifrikya; the most renowned among them was Mussa Ibn Nassir who authorized Tarek Ibn Ziad to conquer Andalusia which became after the conquest a county under the rule of Kairwan and subjoined to it.

During the reign of Harun Arrashid, the khalif of the Abbassides' dynasty in Irak, the people of Kairwan requested that Kairwan should have its autonomy and that Ibrahim Ibn Al Aghlab should be appointed a prince on Kairwan. Harun Arrashid was willing to satisfy their wish and that coincided with his desire to give the Maghreb area their autonomy. So he appointed Ibrahim Ibn Al Aghlab prince of Kairwan provided that the latter paid a yearly duty to the khalifate.

The reign of the Aghlabites over Kairwan lasted 112 years during which eleven kings, the children and grandchildren of Ibrahim Ibn Al Alghlab the founder of the Aghlabites state, reigned successively over Kairwan.

When the Aghlabites' state fell in the year 297, the Ubaidia state (of Shiaa doctrine) succeeded. The Ubaidis' princes reigned over for 65 years. During their reign, Kairwan remained the capital of Ifrikya for the first eleven years, then the capital was transferred to Mahdia (a city in the south east of Tunisia) when Ubaidullah Al Mahdi was crowned king. In fact, Ubaidullah apprehended that the people of kairwan would stand against the Shiaa doctrine. That is why he transferred the government to Mahdia and made the capital of Ifrikya.

There was a period of unrest and trouble in Kairwan. Then when peace and calm were restored after the insurrection of "Sahib Al Himar" and his companions, Al Mansur (an Aghlabite prince) built a city half a mile distant from Kairwan which he called "Al Mansuria" and made it a military base for his rule. That was in the year 336, after which some Sunhaji princes made Kairwan the headquarters of their state until the

Arabs of the Upper Nile in Egypt, called the Hilalyine, marched upon it and destroyed it almost entirely by wiping out its palaces and most of its buildings and monuments, so much so that Kairwan turned into ruins and only its sites remained bespeaking the savagery and cruelty of those aggressive invaders, the Hilalian tribe from Upper Egypt.

To sum up, Kairwan was the first Islamic capital of Ifrikya and Andalusia in the year 95. It was also the military headquarters of the Muslim soldiers and the school for the teaching of Arabic and the dissemination of Islam in Ifrikya where many of the Prophet's Companions had access to, like Abdullah Ibn Abbass, Abdullah Ibn Omar and Abdurrahman, the son of Abu Bakr Issidik, the Prophet's bosom friend and companion, and many other Muslim scholars.

During the reign of the Aghlabites, the domination of Kairwan as being "the capital" of Ifrikya extended to Barka and Tripoli in Libya, Constantine and Algiers in Algeria, and some Meditrranean cities such as, Sardigna in Italy, Malta and Cyprus.

Thus Kairwan reached an outstanding supremacy in civilization and urbanization during the Aghlabites'reign, and this is due to the flow of the Arabs and other races; let not speak of the edification of many buildings and the installment of many institutions and urban and cultural establishments, in addition to the building of many pools whose water was brought to the people of Kairwan from Shrishira and Djelloula (two towns in the outskirts of Kairwan).

Ubaidullah El Bekr, a historian, pointed out that Kairwan had 49 Turkish baths and about 300 mosques. As for the walls which surrounded Kairwan from all sides, they had 14 gates, the most known among them was Abi Rabbis'gate located between the 'Kibla' and the east. To the east of that gate was Okhba Ibn Nafaa's gate and Salam's gate was westward. Unfortunately all those great monuments were entirely wiped out by the Hilalyin; the same happened to the castles, palaces and monuments when Kairwan was devastated. Henceforth, Kairwan lost its glamour and fame as the capital of Ifrikya, and in 449 of the Hegira year, Tunis started to gain a high position and became the capital. However, Kairwan did not lose its spiritual glamour which continued to exist for centuries. In fact, it became the spiritual capital of Islam in North Africa.

*A general view of Abi Zamma Al Baloui's mausoleum,*

One of the Prophet's companions who pledged allegiance to the Prophet (PUB) under the tree. He went on Jihad (holy war), died in Jellula, a town distant 30 kms from Kairwan and was buried in Kairwan.

# The Era of Governors (50- 185 Hegira)

## I. The uprising of the Berbers:

The pre-Islamic era witnessed that Ifrikya was a coveted prey of many conquerors from different races. It was also the victim of disastrous natural and human calamities, and the battlefield of long bloody wars. Its first inhabitants, the Berbers, suffered greatly from unrest and insecurity, and this is due to the fact that the insurrections which broke out everywhere in the country and the injustice of the oppressors at different intervals made the people of Kairwan live continuously in a state of unrest and mutiny. This situation drove them to resort to successive insurrections and rebellions against the rulers depriving the city and its people of peace and calm and plunging the city into chaos and disorder.

It is not unusual then that the Islamic conquest of Ifrikya lasted more than half a century during which the Muslims underwent a lot of sacrifice and lost thousands of people due to the terrific uprisings of the Berbers. Describing those people, Okhba witnessed that the Berbers, who were the people of Kairwan at that time, had no manners or morals. It was only when they were put to the sword that they surrendered, but when the Muslims withdrew, they reverted to their bad customs of killing, destroying and looting.

Soleiman Ibn Abdullah asked one day Moussa Ibn Nassir (a conqueror), "tell me about the Berbers," Moussa answered, "they are rather like the non-Arabs than the Arabs themselves in character and behavior. They are unified, helpful, chivalrous and patient. But they are neither faithful nor trustworthy."

When talking about the uprising of the Berbers, one can give the example of their assault on Okhba and his companions when returning from Uraas Mountains in Algeria, then their advance towards Kairwan in such a big army under the leadership of Kusail that the Arabs found themselves unable to drive them back. This ended with Okhba's withdrawl from Kairwan in company of its prince at that time, Zuhair El Balaoui. Zuhair and his garrison settled outside Kairwan and made a pledge to the Muslims to bring them back peace and safety. When that prince (Zouhair) was backed up with an army from the east, he marched with that army towards Kairwan, and after a fierce attack against the enemy, Kusaila was killed and his army was vanquished. Finally, the Muslims saved their capital, Kairwan, from the Berbers.

When Abdel Malik Ibnu Marwan was nominated Caliph, he pledged to undermine the intrepidity of the Berbers who rallied round a woman leader nicknamed the "priestess". When "the priestess" started to rule, she demanded that all cities and villages in Ifrikya should be devastated, that wells and sources should be dried out, and that trees should be uprooted, believing that all this destruction and devastation would make the Arabs forsake worldly pleasures. Her devilish schemes were eventually carried out. However, Abdel Malik sent a huge army of forty thousand soldiers or so under the command of Hassan Ibn Naamen Al Ghassani, and the two armies met in El Djem (a Roman city in the south east of Tunisia) and a fierce battle broke out ending with the surrender of the priestess, and the defeat of her army. That was in 85 of the Hegira year.

When peace and security were regained, Hassan started to care for the prosperity of the country. He established a shipyard near Carthage for the building of ships. He ordered that all the office books should be written in Arabic, and farmlands be distributed on the small farmers of the Berbers. When the priestess was converted to Islam, he appointed her two sons commanders of the Arab army. Thus did he win the support of the Berbers, and gave them proof that he who converted to Islam would have equal rights and duties as the Arab Muslims. Accordingly many governors from Ifrikya followed this orthodox method when dealing with the Muslim Berbers, until they became more obedient to their governors and more loyal to the country than the Arabs themselves. Eventually, the Berbers were integrated into the Arab nation, and the insurrections and disturbances that had torn Ifrikya before would have gradually subsided should not the venomous seditions that had afflicted the Middle East have infiltrated into Ifrikya.

In fact, the Berbers took advantage of the conflicts between the Arab governors to provoke disturbances anew resorting to what was innate in them, that is their hatred of the outsider and their rebellion against him regardless of his political system. In a word, they adhered to the doctrine of the dissenters which consisted of disobeying the governor in power. The governor at that time was Handhala Ibn Safwan. So instead of rallying around their leader, they rallied around the leader of the opposition Ukhashaa Assafari. Nevertheless Ha    ndhala managed to defeat Ukhashaa and to drive away his followers. Some historians hinted that Ifrikya had not suffered a more fierce battle than the one waged by Handhala during which the casualties numbered one hundred and eighty thousand or so. That terrible war broke out in 124 of the Hegira year.

In the meantime, one of Okhba Ibn Nafaa's grandson called Abdurrahman Ibn Habib Al Fehri rebelled, gathered around him the rebellious Berbers and entered grudgingly Kairwan. Ibn Habib made himself governor and Handhala was compelled to decamp from Kairwan to the Middle East and settled there until the Islamic Caliphate passed on to the Abbasides. Then Jaafar Al Mansur (the Iraki Commander of the Faithful) sent Mohamed Ibn Al Ashaath with forty thousand soldiers to save Ifrikya from the Berbers.

13

One of the most conspicuous mistakes that the Berbers had noticed about the Arabs and which had weakened their position in Ifrikya was when Mouawia ousted Okhba and entrusted Muslima Al Ansari with the government of Egypt and Ifrikya.

Ibn Dinar told that when Muslima arrived in Egypt, he appointed a governor on Ifrikya known as Abi Al Muhajer Dinar. When the latter arrived there, he started disparaging Okhba and his reign over Ifrikya, and he refused to camp in Kairwan where Okhba used to reign. So he marched along with his army away from Kairwan until he had evacuated it almost entirely, built another city and ordered his subjects to live in.

It was due to thoughtlessness and mismanagement that Abi Al Muhajer ventured into that misdeed in order to offend his predecessor in a country where the pioneers and conquerors had hardly stepped in.

As Al Khudari (a historian) put it: "this timeworn deficiency had been so far the cause of the Muslims' sufferings. Instead of profiting by the ideas and experience of his predecessor, the successor endeavored deliberately to belittle and debunk him until his name and his reputation were tarnished and all the extolment passed on to his successor. This is a selfish and futile way of thinking which no nation that would succeed or govern authoritatively dared take into account… Among the most famous governors of Ifrikya in that era, it is worth mentioning:

1. Ubaidullah Ibn Al Habhab who built the Zeituna Mosque in Tunis in the Hegira year 116.

2. Yazid Ibn Hatem Malhabi who renewed the building of Okhba Mosque in Kairwan and ordered the building of a market place in Kairwan by allocating each industry a particular place and that was in the year 157. It was said that one day, while Yazid was on a supervising visit in the outskirts of Kairwan, he saw a flock of sheep and goats, he asked about its owner, he was told that it belonged to his son. He reprimanded him

14

for competing unjustly with the poor farmers and got hold of his flock, thus trying to eradicate all sorts of oppression and injustice by slaughtering all the flock that belonged to his son and he donated its meat to the poor and needy.

*This is the Castle of Monastir (a seaside town in the south east of Tunisia). It used to be a refuge for the hermits and ascetics during the Islamic conquest of Ifrikya.*

## II. The Religious Movement in the Era of Governors:

The Muslim conquerors came from the Arabian Peninsula to this continent (Ifrikya) for an ideal objective, which was its conversion into a continent whose creed is Islam and whose language is Arabic. This change was done slowly and gradually after undergoing serious mishaps for it is not so easy to eradicate an already existing creed from people's hearts and substitute it for something new and unknown. Neither is it possible to remove from people's tongue a language and a dialect which they have been speaking for ages, and replace it by Arabic to become overnight the language of discourse and thought.

If the conversion of the Arabian Peninsula into Islam had been hard and strenuous, the conversion of the Arab Maghreb was harder and more arduous because it was quite far from the heart of the Islamic state, the Medina.

Historians pointed out that many groups of Berbers had embraced Islam in the early years of conquest. They had likewise collaborated with the Arabs during their conquest of the Maghreb and Andalusia. But it was found out that most of them had not embraced Islam. Furthermore, they had taken part in the conquest only out of avidity for the booty or the escape from tribute, or simply out of admiration for the conquerors, the pioneers of the Maghreb and Andalusian conquest.

Abdullah Ibn Yazid reported that the Berbers, from Tripoli to Tanga, had apostatized twelve times, and their belief in Islam steadied only under the reign of Mussa Bin Nassir in the year 95.

When the caliph, Othman Ibn Affaan (the Prophet's fellow) was killed and discord flared up between Ali and Mouaouia , then clashes erupted between, on the one hand, the factions of the Zubeirs and the Allaouis, and the Umayyads and the dissidents on the other. In fact, Ifrikya became in those days an abode for the Arabs who bore vindictive feelings against the Umayyads' political system brought by the Shiites and the dissidents so that the existent disturbances in the East had extended to the Maghreb states making them eventually a birthplace of various political movements and radical political propaganda which could have deviated Islam from its normal course.

An example of political strifes in that era was of Khaled Ibn Hamid Ezannati and Aassem, the dissident, and also the disturbances caused by the Berbers in the second century of the Hegira. All those disturbances were due to the fact that when the Berbers embraced Islam, they did not understand it properly, neither were they convinced by the principles and teachings brought about by Islam. This results into their being lured by any propagandist who disseminated successfully his ideology. When things came back to normal and the conquests were over, the Berbers were eager to understand the true message of Islam by learning first the language through which Islam had been revealed, that is Arabic. But they found out that the Muslim governor was uninterested, with the exception of Omar Ibn Abdel Aziz who sent to Ifrikya ten of his disciples in order to teach people there the precepts of Islam. Unfortunately, those messengers discovered that the Arabs who were settled in Ifrikya or those going there had sectarian tendencies or political aspirations. They also found unpretentious people whose intellectual capacities did not enable them to enlighten those craving for theological studies and scientific knowledge. In fact, the Middle East scholars who went to Ifrikya during the early conquests were versed in theology, but they could not propagate the precepts of Islam as they should have because of the instability and anarchy reigning at that time, so that things lingered until an elite of theologists was formed in the second century and it was they who carried the torch of disseminating Islamic knowledge in Ifrikya. Many of those brave scholars suffered the hardships of the treck to the East in order to learn jurisprudence from well-known scholars like Abdullah Ibn Omar, Abi Huraira, Anas Ibnou Malik and Sofiane Ibn Inaa. Then they returned to the main cities of Ifrikya, such as Kairwan, Soussa and Tunis to teach people Islamic theology and broaden their knowledge in all that had to do with Islamic precepts. Little by little, they formed a new generation of scholars and rhetoricians who played an effective and efficient role as to the propagation of a dynamic scientific and religious activity in Ifrikya. Among the most authoritative adept who set step in Kairwan was Okhba Bin Nafaa.

*The minaret of Okbaa Bin Nafaa's Mosque It is 35 meters high and it has 128 stairs. The Muslim architects in Morocco and Andalusia took this minaret as a specimen to their mosques because it is unparalleled in its magnificence and its glamour*

## III. Okhba Bin Nafaa

Okhba was born in Medina in the first century of the Hegira era. He went to Ifrikya in the year 50 in a huge army. He marched inside an Islamic city which he called "Kairwan". Kairwan is a Persian word used in Arabic, and it means the army camp. In fact, Okhba made of Kairwan an encampment for his army. Then the Caliph Mouaouia Ibn Abi Sofiane appointed him governor in the Middle East and he commissioned in his place Aba Al Muhajir Dinar. During the appointment of Yazid Ibn Mouaouia as a successor, Kairwan became disorganized. So Okhba was made its governor again in the year 62 to put things in order. When he set it right anew, he appointed Zuhair Ibn Kaies Al Balaoui as his successor. After that, he made for Morroco and vanquished the Berbers there after waging a fierce battle against them. It was told that when he reached the Atlantic Ocean, he raised his hands to the sky and invoked God's help in these words: "Will Allah witness that I did my utmost. Weren't the Ocean the great obstacle, I would move further in order to kill those unbelievers and force them to worship none but You, Allah!" Then he traced his way back joining his army which was ahead of him. What is noticeable is that only three hundred soldiers or so were accompanying Okhba during his return to Kairwan, among them was Kusaila, the Berber's leader who was made prisoner then. So he seized the opportunity to inform his tribe, when Okhba and his men were crossing Algeria, of the paucity of the Muslim batallion so that they attacked Okhba's regiment and killed all of them, including Okhba. Okhba was killed near Beskra, an Algerian city, and was buried there in 64 of the Hegira year. Nowadays, the Algerians of that area know him by the name "Sidi Okhba".

What was told about Okhba before his death was the testament he had left for his children in Kairwan before going to the Holy War (Jihad). The testament goes as follows: "Dear sons, I have sacrificed myself for the sake of God, and only God knows what might happen to me during my journey.

I recommend that you take into consideration these high moral precepts and try not to ignore or neglect them. Fill your hearts with the reading of Allah's Book (the Koran) which is an evidence of God's pre-eminence and omnipresence. Emulate the discourse of the Arabs so that your tongues will be rightly guided and you will be taught the noble manners of the Arabs. I likewise advise you not to fall into the trap of debt even though you keep wearing shabby clothes because debt leads to anxiety at night and baseness in the day. Do not take knowledge from those who are pretentious because they may discard you from God. Do not learn religious precepts but only from those who fear God and this is safer to you, and only those who are precautious will be salvaged and will live in quietude!"

## IV. Abu Abderrahman Al Habli

His real name is Abdullah Bin Yazid Al Maarifi. He went to Kairwan at the head of a delagation made up of ten legal scholars chosen and sent by the Commander of the Faithful, Omar Ibnu Abdel Aziz to Ifrikya to teach people there Islamic jurisprudence.

Habli used to be a narrator of Hadith (Prophetic Tradition) which he had learnt from a group of the Prophet's Companions, like Abu Ayub Al Ansari and Abdullah Ibn Omar. Al Habli lived in Kairwan where he built a mosque next to Tunis Gate (name given to one of the seven gates in Kairwan) which he called "Al Ansar mosque". He died in Kairwan and his tomb could be seen in an area called, "Hattabia".

What is to be remembered was his famous declaration: "the example of the one who averts great sins and falls in baseness is like the example of someone who comes face to face with a panther and stands on his guards against its danger in order to be safe, then when an ant bites him, he ignores it, and when another ant comes and bites him, he shows his indifference to it until all the ants join forces against him and kill him in the end."

## V. Abdurrahman Ibn Ziyad Al Maariffi

He was born in Kairwan in 64 of the Hegira year. His father had been among those who came to Ifrikya in company of Okhba Bin Nafaa. Abdurrahman grew up in quest of knowledge until he became a narrator of Hadith (the Prophet's tradition), a litrary man and a poet. He was well-known for his asceticism and piety. Besides, he was inseparable from Abu Jaafar Al Mansur (an Iraki caliphate) before he was made his successor. He returned to Kairwan, and once again made for Irak. He went to see Abu Jaafar when he was a caliph. The latter asked him: "Could you tell me what you saw hidden behind our doors?" Al Maarifi answered: "I saw only deep darkness," then he added, "the nearer I came, the darker it became." "You're absolutely right to claim this to us, and your claim is welcome," Abu Jaafar replied. "To tell the truth, your sultanate has become like a black market," Al Maarifi put in. "You look as if you've started to dislike our companionship." Abu jaafar remarked. "Not at all. Honor and richness are only reached through your companionship" Al Maarifi retorted.

Abu Abdurrahman Al Maarifi was made twice the magistrate of Kairwan. He died in the year 161 and he was buried in Kairwan graveyard near Naffa's gate.

## VI. Hansh Assanaani

He was well-known among the hadith narrators. He took the Hadith amongst a Group of the Prophet's Companions, like Imam Ali, the Prophet's cousin, Ibn Omar, Ibn Abass. He was born in Sanaa, Yemen. He witnessed the conquest of Ifrikya and the conquest of Andalusia under the command of Mussa Ben Nassir. Then he returned to Kairwan and lived there until his death in 100. His tomb was built next to Abi Zamaa Al Balaoui's,( the Prophet's follower and barbar). Hansh was so charitable that hardly did he dismiss a beggar when he asked for almonds, or when a beggar knocked at the door of his house, he said calling at a high voice the servants or the inmates to bring him food. "Give food to the beggar until he's satiate."

## VII. Bahlul Ibn Rashid

Born in Kairwan in the year 128, he was taught theology by Malek Ibnu Anass in Medina. Talking about Bahlul, Anass said: "this fellowman is a great lover of his native town, Kairwan." When Bahlul returned from Medina to Kairwan, he taught Imam Sahnun, one of the most famous theologians of Kairwan, theology which proved out to be of great use to Sahnun.

"A little science in a competent man is like the fresh water of a water stream in a fertile land whose owner will profit by its crops" he would say when alluding to Imam Sahnun. "He is a virtuous man well versed in jurisprudence.

Bahlul Ibn Rashid died in the Hegira year 183 and he was buried next to Salam gate in Kairwan, and his tombstone is still there.

# The Aghlabites' era (185–296)

During their reign, the Aghlabites were considered the masters of the Mediterranean. Their governance was strengthened and their power extended up to Barka and Tripoli in Libya and Constantine in Algeria. The Alghlabites built a strong fleet with which they succeeded to conquer Sicily, Malta and Sardigna. Furthermore, in order to protect their city, Kairwan, from sea invasion, forts and walls were built and safeguarded by jurists, ascetic people and devotees. Some of the monuments they had built are still there, like the forts and walls they had built in Hammamet and Kelibia (in the north east of Tunisia). They also surrounded sea-shore cities, like Monastir and Soussa, with well-fortified walls, some of which are still standing unassailable. Likewise a newly built up city known as Abbassia was edified three miles away from Kairwan, and another city known as Rakadda was built six miles away from Kairwan. These two cities are suburbian to Kairwan. The king at that time, known as Ibrahim Ibn Aghlab, could not sleep at night because Kairwan is very hot. He built his palace in Rakkada because he was told that the atmosphere there made one who suffered from insomnia sleep well. The Aghlbites built also fabulous palaces, hotels, Turkish baths, mosques and lighthouses. We can give the example of Ibn Khairun mosque in Kairwan and Sidi Bou Saiid lighhouse in the north east of Tunis. As for the outstanding architecture for which the Aghlabites were known, we can mention as an example of illustration the minaret of Okhba mosque with its marble punctured niche and the elaborately ornated pulpit of the same mosque.

## I. The Aghlabites'policy

The Aghlabites'era was known for its domination over the Mediterranean. Their state was enlarged stretching out to Berka, Tripoli in Libya and Cosstantine to Algiers. Their developed political system made them care for the rivival of the rural areas. Their giving great importance to irrigation had them bring spring and valley waters to cisterns and pools which they had built in order to collect these waters for the irrigation of thousands of acres of farmland. Many of these pools and cisterns are still extant nowadays in places like Rakkada, or what is known nowadays as the Aghlabites' pools in the northwestern outskirts of Kairwan. One can also mention Merdin pool near Msaken and Saffra cistern in Soussa. Irrigation water was collected in such great quantity in those huge containers to irrigate acres and acres of farmlands surrounding Kairwan in such a way that agriculture prospered, not only in Kairwan, but also in the whole central parts of Tunisia, and more particularly in the suburbs of Kairwan which had become, as historians described them, the paradisiacal areas of Tunisia with the fascinating greenness of their thick fruitful trees and the fragrant and sweet smelling flowery gardens.

Industry had also flourished in that age. In fact, markets were built and workshops were established to make various kinds of weapons and gunpowder. Other worshops specialised in the making of glass, crystal, chinaware, painted ceramics, pottery, parchment and scrolls, textiles and embroidery, hide tanning, shoe and saddle making. So trade became so prosperous that it made Kairwan an interesting business center and a stopping place for caravans and merchants, and this is because the Aghlabites'state provided enough transportation and security. Ibn Al Athir, a historian described the situation at that time stating that "caravans and tradesmen would move around in total security."

This edifying policy "enabled the whole country to flourish and to prosper, and particularly Kairwan whose population had doubled both by the growing number of its inhabitants and by those who emigrated to it in such a way that its population reached five hundred thousand. Ibn Khaldun, the great Tunisian historian wrote: "urban life had become the rule in Kairwan and Korduba, the two cities of the Maghreb and Korduba so much so that both science and business became the two outstanding features of the two cities. In fact, workshops, flourishing markets, and abounding seas prevailed, let not speak of the development of education that started spreading progressively all over the country. Those heydays lasted as long as the lasting of a civilized and urbanised life that marked those two cities, Kairwan and Korduba"

## II. The city of Rakkada

The city of Rakkada lies in the south west, about eight miles away from Kairwan. Ibrahim Ibnu Ahmed Al Aghlab built Rakkada in the hegira year 263 because he wanted it to be the residence and headquarters of the Aghlabites' kings. The Abbassia, city situated in the outskirts of Kairwan (3 miles away) looked in his view unbecoming for his rank because the Aghlabites' powerful state turned in those days a state of affluence and extended sultanate, although it did not compete in power and prestige the capitals of great kingdoms in the east like Samarra founded by Mootassam Al Abassi in Irak and Kataai city founded by Ahmed Bin Taloon in Egypt.

Ibrahim Ibn Al Aghlab chose Rakkada for residence and government because of its fresh air and the fertility of its land. Al Bakir, a historian, describing Rakkada said that, "scarcely does one find in Ifrikya a fresher air, a gentler breeze and a more fertile land than in Rakkada."

While planning the new city (Rakkada), Ibrahim Ibn Al Aghlab surrounded it with brushwood and gardens, bringing water to it from distant places and stored it in huge cisterns in case of drought. He fortified Rakkada with strong walls, and just in the middle, he built a mosque whose marble pillars were brought from Sicily, in the south of Italy. Then he built a palace for himself which he called, "the palace of wisdom", and next to it he built what he called, "the house of wisdom". That shows the great interest that king gave to knowledge and science at that time. Ibrahim Ibn Al Aghlab also built many other palaces, like "the patio palace" and "Baghdad palace".

Ibrahim Ibn Al Aghlab did not make of Rakkada only a residential or government city for himself and for his retinue, but he also built in it markets, hotels, Turkish baths, and every commodity of life so that it became eventually after a few years a citadel abounding in riches and welfare. Historians stated that the young king allowed the sale of wine which was entirely forbidden in Kairwan. This made the poets of the time write in protest, "You lord of the people and son of the lords, whose people are their slaves, what makes you allow the drinking of wine in Rakkada and forbid it in our prestigious city, Kairwan."

Rakadda remained for long the abode of the Aghlabites until Ziadatu Allah Al Akhir took over in the Higira year 293. He built for himself a palace and called it "The Sea Palace." Some of its walls are still standing, but one of the inhabitants of the area built on it a house, and that was in the 1950s before the Independence of Tunisia;

The Aghlabites liked to be freed from living in Rakadda. So in 296 Ziadetou Allah Al Akhir left Rakkada for the Middle East, and Ubaida Allah Al Mahdi, coming from Mahdia (in the south east of Kairwan) established his headquarters in Rakadda. Thus Rakadda became the headquarters of the Ubaida state in the Hegira year 308.

Nowadays Rakadda was vivified after a long period of stagnation. Water springs gushed forth. People started growing all sorts of fruit trees, and the population began to increase. That was after centuries of total slumber when centuries of florescence and development that Rakkada had lived were entirely forgotten. In the early1960s, president Bourguiba built a palace there trying to revive the flourishing civilization that Rakadda had known with the Aghlabites. Archeologists were ordered to make their excavation in search of what was left of the wrecked ruins. They discovered the remains of Roman graveyards containing a lot of earthenware. They also unearthed many Aghlabites' rarities which were exhibited in Ibrahim Ibn Al Aghlabs'Antiquities Museum in Kairwan.

*The Aghlabites'pool*

It was founded by Ibrahims'father, Ahmed Ibn Al Aghlab in the Hegira year, 245. Next to this pool is a small one in which water was collected from water springs in Shrishira and Jelloula through curves. The water was used by the inhabitants of Rakadda and Kairwan for the irrigation of their gardens and orchards. In the middle of the big pool can be seen a seat built for the Aghlabites'king to sit in when he went for an outing in the outskirts of Kairwan. This same seat was used by president Bourguiba on the Muled (the Prophet's birthday) in 1963. A platform was built on the seat and boats were brought down into the pool to carry the president and his retinue up to the platform to sit and listen to music played by a folkloric orchestra.

## IV. The scholastic activity in the Aghlabites'era

Education spread out in the Aghlabites'era thanks to the implementation of koranic schools (kataatib) in Kairwan and in other cities in Ifrikya where children were taught the holy Koran, the basics of Arabic language and the precepts of Islam. In addition to the koranic schools, the Aghlabites founded mosques that taught theology, like the interpretation of the Koran and the Hadith (the Prophet's sayings), jurisprudence, linguistics and philology including grammar, morphology and poetry.

Ibnu Naji, a historian, told about the characteristics of Islam at that time, saying that "Abdullah Ibn Ghanem left the Big Mosque in Kairwan, known also by the name of his founder, Okba Bin Nafaa, after one Friday prayer, and a short time after, one of his fellows called on. Ibn Ghanem asked him "were you at the mosque?" "Yes, I

was." Answered his friend. "What did you see?" Was Ibn Ghanem's question. "I saw seventy caps whose bearers would be judges and three hundred caps whose bearers would be jurists." Ibn Ghanem remarked sorrowfully, "people are dead."

He implied that the number of scholars was much reduced compared to what it had been years ago. However, the number of scholars mentioned by Ibn Ghanem's friend showed how great the number of scholars was at that time. Besides, what contributed to the increase of Knowledge at that time was people's attendance in great number to the various lectures given on subjects, like jurisprudence, prophetic discourse, let not speak of the prestige and high position that the scholars had enjoyed in Ifrikya's society, and also the scholars'immigration from the Middle East to Ifrikya and vice versa.

In the second century of the Hegira year,many of the Kairwan scholars immigrated to Damascus, Baghdad, Basra and Kufa. Some of them made for the Medina in the Arabian Peninsula and learned from Imam Malek Ibn Annas and so became his disciples. Then they returned to Kairwan teaching people what they had learned. Some others were taught by Imam Malek's students like Kassed Ibn Al Furat, Bahlul Ibn Rashid and many others. Malek was greatly interested in his pupils, inquiring about them after their return to Kairwan. He was continuously in touch with them through letter writing. When he died, his pupils, like Ibn Al Kassem, Ashab and Ibn Wahb became the cynosure of young scholars in Kairwan and Ifrikya. They compiled what they had learned from their teacher Malek, and they started writing books in jurisprudence and Islamic philosophy for people to read, emulating Malek's approach in his dealing with these subjects and others. One can give the example of Imam Sahnun (a well-known jurist and thinker at that time) who was Malek's most faithful disciple.

The mystery behind Kairwan jurists' and thinkers' devotion to Malek's school of teaching, their being staunch defenders of his doctrine, and their aversion to Irak's jurists like those adhering to Imam Hanaafi's doctrine, is that Hanaafi'spupils relied on rigid reasoning, and they coined far-fetched verdicts; let not speak of their excessive love for princes and their searching for insensible interpretation of religious texts in order to find out permissions for the princes to act sometimes against religious regulations. All this made Malek's disciples stay away from Imam Hanaafi's doctrine..

Besides, the jurists of Kairwan, advocators of Malek's ideology, believed that the safety of creed lay in its being protected from the Iraki immoderate 'Shiaa' and the rebellious Dissidents (known as Al Khaouarij) who started spitting out their venom in Ifrikya, The Malikis considered the Shiaa and Dissidents originating from the Omayaads and the Abassides dynasty as enemies of Islam. However, those radical Shiaa and rebellious Dissidents became so powerful that they began to stand against Malik's sunnists because of their objective opinion and their constructive interpretation of the Koran and the Hadith, and they criticized them harshly with their slanderous defamation considering that any deviation from their immoderate dissidence was like apostasy.

It is because of all these extremely dark ideas that when Imam Sahnun became a jurist refused to accept the teaching of 'Abadhya', 'Safriaa', and 'Mootazilaa' (they were Shiaa sects whose ideology was based on radical reasoning) in koranic schools or in mosques, and particularly the Big Mosque in Kairwan, known also by the name of Okba Mosque. He also refused the members of those sects to be appointed Imams in mosques or to be teachers in schools. Sehnun prohibited any debates and discussions that were ouside Malek's jurisprudence.

This religious rigidity on the part of the Malikis presented obviously many inconveniences like closing horizons that could have broadened the mind and penting up talents that could have arisen. Furthermore,this religious coercion had restricted minds that could have been freed, thus narrowing people's understanding of religion. However, one should not deny the advantages that this religious restrictness had at that time politically and religiously, such as the unification of forces, the agreement of effort in an era when Ifrikya hardly became an arena of political greed and sectarian conflict. In fact, this area had suffered a lot from political secession many years before Islam, and this secession had consequently been the cause of a wide variance in customs and traditions, beliefs and differences in languages and dialects. So Malek's doctrinal activity acted like a political party unifying people under its banner, saving them from dissension and dissolution.

One should also take into consideration the fact that the Aghlabites'princes did not conform to Malek's orientation; neither did they give any importance to Malek's zealotry which the people and scholars of Kairwan were very proud of. However, the princes paradoxically took their advisory opinion and rules of law from Iraki scholars and jurists so that conflicts broke out often between the two schools, the Iraki and Malek's. Some of the princes sometimes felt that the opposing attitude they were taking caused such a fierce defiance of the people against their government. This pushed them to react so cruelly against some Maliki scholars, persecuting and imprisoning them sometimes unjustly, making of them real martyrs who deserved great respect and dignity from their advocators who considered them as the victims of injustice and the wrong interpretation of Islam.

Thus the Maliki scholars in Kairwan gained the sympathy and support of thousands of new followers and their opposition to the government had such an impact on the laity who believed that the Maliki system of life was entirely Islamic and devoid of hypocrisy because it was in keeping with the rules and regulations of religion. Furthermore, the Maliki scholars did not use religion as a means for political ambitions as the scholars of the other sects did. Contrarily, Malek advised his pupils to keep faith away from any worldly objective stating that "a scholar should stand as far as possible, body and soul, from sultans, governors and men of power. He should not have any contact with them lest he be tempted by their riches and power." So most of the scholars used to observe strictly Malek's recommendations.

Mohamed Sehnun, son of Imam Sehnun said to his father one day, "Mr. so and so went to see the governor at night so that people would not see him. Some of his brethren wrote to him these words: "He who sees you in the day can see you at night, (meaning God)." Imam Shnun was impressed by these words adding, "how disgraceful a scholar becomes when people go to attend his lecture but they do not find him. When they inquire about his whereabouts, they are informed that he went to see the prince or the minister. So if you feel that a scholar is fond of life and is tempted by the lurid attractions of a king or a prince, you had better keep away from him because he is no longer worth the title of a scholar."

Imam Sehnun played undoubtedly a major turn in order to make public Malek's doctrine and consolidate it in Ifrikya so that this doctrine began to have such an impact on the social and political life of the time. Malek's doctrine became the only doctrine followed in Infriya and this is due to Sehnun's wise way of disseminating it among the laity. He managed at the same time to expound Malek's own precepts, his system of life and his position towards many laws so that many scholars took them posthumously as a line of conduct.

In fact, Sehnun was an example of life to many scholars who considered him as a leader and proponent of Malek's doctrine. He would state repeatedly in the lectures he gave to his pupils or to the laity that "the Imams should always be respected and their views should be taken for granted. They should not be attacked or transgressed even if they deviate sometimes from truth." He also believed that "revolutions and seditions could cause disturbances in the government and they could end with calamity and disaster that would serve only the enemy."

Nevertheless, these declarations did not prevent Sehnun's and of course Malek's disciples from declaring publicly their support of truth and their peaceful opposition to the government when a prince or a king swerved from faith, but their opposition was entirely free from any personal or political greed. Therefore, their disinterest for power helped them keep away from rank or position and made them live in peace, mutual love and stick together in weal and woe.

Now what justifies people's taking interest more in theology than in linguistics or other specialities was that theology was much needed at that time for the graduation of jurists from whom magistrates were selected. This post was very important and it was closely connected with people's business and their problems. The Aghlabites' kings used to meet with the think tank of the state to seek their advice as to the appointment of a magistrate. In fact, since people began to realize the magnificence of this post, they used all possible means to convince the prince to appoint or dismiss a magistrate as was the case of the dismissal of Ibn Abi Al Jaoued and the appointment of Imam Sehnun instead.

However, the Aghlabites' princes would rather appoint Kufi jurists (those who were taught in Kufa, Irak). Those jurists were often of the Hanafi sect and not the Maliki's). They worked in favor of the prince and not of the people. Nevertheless, the Maliki jurists were more successful in their jobs. In fact, the difference was so great between Maliki magistrates who advised the prince to be more dutiful and more benevolent towards the people, and to keep a close eye on his subordinates, dismissing those who were unjust or tyranical, but a Kufi magistrate was servile to the prince and he always complained to him of those who despised him or rebelled against him.

## IV. The most well-known scholars in the Aghlabites'era

### 1. Assaad Ibn Al Furat:

He was a native of Khorassan (a country in the previous Soviet Union), but he was reared and educated in Kairwan. He accompanied the governor Mohamed Ibn Al Ashaath to Kairwan, and he studied in Tunis. His teacher was Ali Ibn Ziyad. He travelled to Medina in the Arabian Peninsula where he was taught by Imam Ibn Malek. Then he made for Irak and he learned from Abi Youssef, a Hanafi theologist and jurist, and a friend of Abi Hanafi who set thousands of questions on Islam and Islamic law. Those questions were eventually turned into rules of law. Assad freed the questions from those rules of law and submitted them to Malek. Then he wrote down those questions in his book. It was said that the book contained thirty six thousand questions. He called the book "Al Assadia". After publishing his book, he returned to Kairwan, started teaching, and many people graduated from his school with Imam Sehnun at the head. In 204, he was appointed a magistrate over the whole of Ifrikya. When Ziyad Ibn Al Aghlab decided to invade Sicily, Assad asked to make him a soldier, but the latter made him the commander of the army that invaded Sicily. "I will appoint you the prince of Sicily, and I will not dismiss you from the position of a magistrate. So you will be both a prince and a magistrate," he said to him.

Al Assad left out from the seaport of Soussa at the head of ten thousand soldiers and landed at the coast of Sicily. He came to grips with the Sicilians, and immediately the war broke out. Assad fought desparately in many places until he martyred when he was wounded seriously in the town of Saracussa, the capital of Sicily, and he was buried there. That was in 213.

Al Assad was asked about the advantages of wine. He declared that wine is the worst impurity, and it must be absolutely prohibited during the prayers and during fasting. He who indulges in drinking will not be admitted into Paradise. Besides, neither his holy fighting nor his charitable works will be accepted. Then he added sarcastically, drinking is only permissable for those who play the luth or the bagpipe and the drums.

Abdel Khalek Al Mutaabed, his friend and disciple asked him one day, "Abu Abdullah, how is it that you start to depend more on your personal opinion than on the Prophetic tradition and the tradition of your predecessors?" Assad answered: "Don't you know that the Prophet's Companions' utterances are nothing but personal opinion at first , and then they become a tradition after their death. The same thing can be applied to their disciples; that is, what they utter is something personal which consequently becomes a tradition after their death. What Al Assad wants to say is that one should not stick to the tradition of the predecessors, because one's opinion is as valuable as the predecessors'traditon.

*The niche of Okhba Ben Nafaa Mosque*

It was built in the reign of Ziadatou Allah Al Aghlabi. The wall of this niche is decorated with 130 pieces of ceramics on which are drawn a variety of multi-shaped designs, whose metallic pieces glow like the glistening of gold.

Inside the niche lies white-covered and perforated marble.

## 2. Imam Suhnun

His name was Abdussalem Ibn Saied. He was born in Kairwan in the Hegira year 160. He learned theology in Ifrikya from Assad Ibn Al

Furat. Then he moved to the Middle East and visited Al Hijaz (Mecca and Medina), Egypt and Shaam (Syria and Palestine). His tutors were Abul Kassem, Ibn Wahab and other learned men who were themselves Malek's disciples. He read over and over what Al Assad Ibn Al Furat had written about Abul Kassem's manuscripts and he rectified and rewritten them. The he returned to Kairwan and wrote "The Manuscript" which found a great demand from the readership, not only in Kairwan, but also in Morocco and Andalusia.

Sehnun was considered an unparalleled theologian and jurist by propagating Malek's doctrine in Ifrikya. Besides, many scholars graduated from his school. Ibnu Naji, a historian confirmed that Imam Sehnun graduated more than 700 scholars. Abu Al Arab, another historian wrote that those who attended Sehnun's lectures were more from the laity than from the learned men. Many of his students came from different parts of Ifrikya, Sicily and Andalusia.

When Sehnun became a celebrity, prince Abul Abass Ahmed Ibnu Al Aghlab was told that people started venerating and glorifying Imam Sehnun. So he prevented him indirectly from fulfilling his duty as a scholar by appointing him a judge over all Ifrikya in the year 234. But Sehnun refused this position many times. He declared his refusal in these words: "I don't see any good to accept this post, but in order to convince me to accept it, the prince allowed me absolute freedom in my judgement. I said to him that I am going to begin by judging his kinship and subordinates who were actually very corrupt and quite unjust towards the people and the state by embezzling a lot of money from the state's treasure and plundering a lot of people's assets, and the prince agreed. In fact the judge who preceded me did not dare to deal with them." Then he added, "the prince confided to me that he had taken much time to think of nominating a righteous and honest judge, and he could not find better than me. When I heard this truth coming out of the mouth of a prince, I could not refuse his request and so accepted the new post."

The first thing to attract the attention of Suhnun, the judge, were the markets. He noticed that they were disordered and lawless. So he decided to put some order in them. Usually, the markets were under the supervision of the governors and not the judges, but since Sehnun was given unlimited freedom to act, he was allowed to take the supervision of the markets under his responsibility. He confided them to superintendents and trusted them with the people's goods and money. He punished swindlers, imposters and speculators. He made a room which he had built in the Big Mosque (Okhba Mosque) as a court of justice for the Maliki judges. So when the judges were Hanafi (adopting Abu Hanifa doctrine), the room was pulled down, and when the judges were Maliki, it was built again.

Sehnun was never afraid to be just in his verdicts even towards those who held power. He convicted so petilessly the oppressors among the people of power that one day they lodged complaints against him at the prince's court. He was summoned to the prince's court, and the prince spoke to him in these words: "Sehnun, I know they are rude, meaning the men of power, and your protecting yourself from their mischief is better than standing always firm against them. Besides, many judges like you trust the conviction of this man to an attorney."

Sehnun replied: "when these oppressors are summoned to the court to be prosecuted, it is a good way to deter them from transgressing the law and from aggressing the others just out of arrogance and haughtiness."

These are some of Suhnun's sayings:

"He whose worldly life is not righteous, his after-life will be marred and deteriorated."

"The wretched man is he who sold his after-life for the sake of this worldly life. But the most wretched one is he who sold his after- life for the sake of someone's worldly life."

Sehnun died in the year 240 and all Kairwan vibrated by the news of his death. Many poets of Kairwan eligized his death, like Abdel Malek Ibn Nassr when he said in his eligy:

"Will God bestow on thee His Blessing and his Grace. Will thou harvest in Paradise what thou sowed in this life."

Mohamed Ibn Al Hareth wrote the most eloquent and elaborate biography on Suhnun.

Suhnun came to Ifrikya imbued with Malek's doctrine. So he combined the advantages of religion with piety and virtuousness. He was actually a boon for the Muslims. People at that time venerated him. His age was like a nascence that had wiped out all that came before. His disciples and friends were of the most highborn families of Kairwan. His son was a prestigious jurist. Ibn Ghafek was the wizard of Kairwan. Ibn Oman was her custodian. Ibn Jibillah was her zealously ascetic person. Kairwan boasted of other noble men. Hemdiss was a staunch traditionalist, sticking to the Prophet's Hadith, and a bitter enemy of heresy. As for Ibn Al Haddad, he was her (Kairwan) most eloquent rhetorician. Ibn Meskin was the narrator of the Prophet's Hadith and the holy books. So all these famous people were Sehnun's friends and disciples.

*The pulpit of Okhba Mosque*

It is one of the most fascinating Aghlabite's work of art. It is made up of three hundred pieces of teak wood on which are carved wonderful patterns of multidinous decorations. This magnificient pulpit is a reference to many designs and drawings found in the famous Kairwan carpets.

### 3. Isaac Ibnu Omran

He was originally from Baghdad. He was of Islamic faith. He was asked to come to Ifrikya by prince Ziyadatu Allah Ibn Al Aghlab, and the latter reassured him that he could return to his country whenever he wished.

He was a skilled doctor with a great experience in the mixing of drugs and the diagnosis of diseases. It was thanks to him that medicine made its appearance in the Maghreb. He settled in Kairwan and wrote scores of books on medicine such as his well-known book entitled, "Relaxation and Recreation". Another book entitled, "An item of drugs". A third book bears the title of "phlebotomy", and a fourth book called, "The pulse". He compiled in another book the opinions of Apocrates and Galinos on "Wine drinking".

It was told that Issaac warned prince Ziadatuallah Ibnu Al Aghlab from drinking a kind of suspicious milk because he was suffering from Asthma, but an Israeli doctor relieved his worry, and he drank from that milk. At night, he fell into a fit of asthma; he became so ill that he was on the verge of death. So he sent for Issaac to cure him, but Issaac refused claiming that he didn't observe his recommendations. He only accepted after being given a thousand riyals.When the prince recovered, he said: "Issaac had sold my soul; I order that his livelihood should be suspended. When his livelihood was suspended by the prince, Issaac went to a spacious square in town and began writing medical prescriptions to the public in exchange for money. The prince was informed about that, he ordered Issaac to be sent to prison. People went to see him there and he continued writing prescriptions for them. When the prince heard about that, he ordered that Issaac should be killed and crucified. Before he was crucified, Issaac told the prince: "You are called the lord of the Arabs, but you are not. Some time ago, I gave you a drug that had harmed terribly your mind."

*The Three-door Mosque*

It was built in Kairwan by Mohammed Ibn Khairoun Al Maarifi Al Andalusi in the year 252. Its minaret was built later. The prayer hall was renovated, but its sculptured façade was kept as it was.

## V. The literary movement

Ifrikya'people were not as versed in literature as in religious matters in the Aghlabites' era, and this is due to the fact that thinkers at that time were more inclined towards theological matters than literary subjects because they felt that Ifrikya had still a greater need for the expansion of Islamic teachings than for anything else. So people reconstructed their lives on religious precepts, let not speak of the great respect they bore for their scholars and for the narrators of the Prophet's (PUB) Hadith. Hence their poetry was predominated by the Islamic ideolgy and thoughts of their scholars. Their poetry dealt with topics like ascetism and mysticism or Soufism. This reminds us of Abu Al Attaia's poetry which is almost religiously committed. In fact, most poetry written in Ifrikya was committed; it was not as free as poetry in the Middle East which rose loftily free over all sorts of commitment roving high in the boundless skies of poetic emotions and feelings of love and passion.

The Ifrikyan poet remained strongly committed to a social and religious environment in which prevailed an atmosphere of austerity, ascetism, traditionalism and soufism; this shows how religion had an overwhelming impact on people's feeling and mind, disposition and even lifestyle. For example, eligiac poetry prevailed so much over all poetic genres that the poetic genius seemed to be prompted only by scenes of death and calamities. When an Ifrikyan poet started writing a poem, he became first unconsciously freed from the bonds of religion and society, but once he felt that he went astray singing the beauty of life and nature, he quickly regained consciousness and he started to disparage life, advising people to forget about the illusiory temptations of this worldly life and to follow a life of mysticism and austerity.

## 1. Bakir Ibnou Hamad:

Abu Isaahk Arrakik, a narrator, told that the poet, Bakir Ibnou Hamad often sought the help of Ibrahim Ibn Al Aghlab and eulogized him with outstanding panegyric poems. He once went to the prince's palace in Rakkada with a praising poem. He asked Ballagh, the prince's servant about the prince. He was told that the prince was having an delightful time with the maid singers in the palace gardens and he did not want to be bothered by the presence of anyone else. The poet, Bakir, improvised some lines that he wrote on a piece of parchment and handed it over to the servant boy to bring to the prince. The lines went on as follows. Addressing the prince he wrote:

"You have created the maid singers to be the cause of affliction for men. They are made to be our masters and we are their servants.

Whenever we wish to have roses any time, their rosy cheeks are there for us to smell."

The parchment reached the prince. He read it, then he handed it over to the maid singers. They enjoyed the reading of these lines, and made them into a nice song. Then they pleaded for the poet, and the prince sent him eventually a purse of one hundred riyals.

However, the poet Bakir suddenly broke up his relations with the past which he considered "dark with evil" and turned overnight into a preacher and sermonizer, renouncing worldly pleasures and reminding his readers of death and life after death.

He wrote in one poem the following:

"Do visit the abodes of those who can never visit us. We have become indeed heedless about how much they are suffering in their graves. Could they speak, they would say, woe to you! Think about what you should bring with you. Your passing away is quite near, and this is what you never wish for. What good worldly life is for those who stick to it. It is no good at all even for those who have collected all the riches of the world." . And then he wrote in another poem:

"... Now you see man full of joy and happiness, then you see him lying on stretchers or in a coffin... This is poor Bakir, (lamenting his fate), life is embittered and spoilt. All of us are on our guards waiting for the last journey and all of us are decamping... Everyday we see a coffin and we escort one, bidding farewell to those who have passed away... Death destroys what we have built in delight and enjoyment... So what are you, poor Bakir waiting for?"

This exaggerated pessimism and asceticism is not the feature of this poet only, but of most of the poets of the time who started their poetry with flirtation and philandering, then turned to God and mysticism. They quickly felt that they became powerless, and that they were withering and shrivelling like a dead flower.

The image of the Ifrikyan poet is like a mirror to the religious and austere environment that Kairwan was living at that time, through which one can see people's view of life much influenced by the dictates of religion and of the scholars than the delighful pleasures of life, with the exception, of course, of princes.

## 2. Ghalboun Ibnou Hassan:

Another good example of a poet that reflects perfectly the atmosphere in which lived the poets of Kairwan at that time is that of the poet Ghalboun Ibn Hassan. Although born in a princely household, surrounded by a life of opulence and lavishness, he turned finally into a mystic shunning worldly life and taking refuge in an austere and morally strict life. However, Ghalboun Bin Hassan, like his predecessors, was at first an impudent poet, and he was much infatuated by women. He would attend every wedding disguised as a woman in order to look closely at women and admire their beauty. Then he turned overnight into a pious man denying worldly life while he was still in the prime of life. He immigrated to Mecca and devoted himself to worshipping God. When his sister entreated him to return to Kairwan to see him before he died, he wrote to her these words: "I will never leave a country where I feel God near me, and come back to a country in which I used to disobey God." Finally, it was his sister who went to Mecca and stayed with her brother. Whe he died, she wrote on his tomb: "Oh brother, there is no reason why I would not go mad after your death. How many inhumed corpses had rotten, but grief will never wear away."

These are some lines of mystic poetry written by Ghalboun:

"Although not satiated, I feel satisfied with whatever victuals I have, but I am entranced to feel that God is my support. Kings and wealthy people appear in my eyes as the basest people. No life is better to me than self satisfaction, and no better food is to me than piety."

To conclude, we can say that the most common poetry in the Aghlabites'era is mystic and eligiac poetry. However, there was another kind of poetic genre at that time; it was eulogistic poetry, in which the poet eulogizes himself or others. In the case of eulogistic poetry in the Arab world at that time, it was often the poet who eulogized a king, a prince or a rich man in order to gain a reward or money.

## 3. Eulogistic poetry:

This is what the prince, Ibrahim Ibnou Al Aghlab, wrote praising his power and determination:

"When I set on my mind to speak to people and convince them, it is with lucidity and clarity that I attain my goal. I am as eloquent and lucid as darkness is made lucid in a rising full moon."

### a. Aissa Ibnu Meskin:

He was an eminent scholar and poet in Kairwan. He was a disciple of Imam Sahnoun. He immigrated to the Middle East and learned at the most distinguished theologians of the time, then returned to Kairwan spreading knowledge among the learned and the laity. He invited people to be wise and benevolent. In addition to having a deep knowledge in theology, he was an inborn poet. He was assigned the responsibility of a magistrate during the reign of Ibrahim Ibn Al Aghlab. He died at the age of eighty and was buried in Kairwan. These are some of the maxims that he wrote:

1.  He who leads a life of indulgence will end up in sorrow.

2.  He who preserves his desire will deserve people's respect and love.

3. Try to be compatible with people's thinking and way of life in order to avoid their injustice and their malevolence.

This is a poem in which the poet, Aissa Ibn Meskin, bemoans young people's life and the passing of youth:

"By my Eternal God, Had I been able to capture my youth anew, I wouldn't have let it escape from me…I missed my youth, and with it I missed my sweetest sleep and I missed the delights of my life, too."

## b. Ahmad Ibnu Souleiman Arribii

Born in Kairwan in 204 and died in 291. He was reared in the learning of Arabic and poetry. Then he engaged in the study of jurisprudence from Imam Sehnun and from prestigious scholars. He kept in close contact with Imam Sehnun for twenty years so much so that he became influenced by his manners and by his noble character. Besides, mysticism and piety prevailed over his behavior and conduct of life.

When Imam Sehnun died, he eligized him in a poem which starts as follows:

"The death of Mohamed was heart-rending and my grief is so deep that it banished my sleep and turned me into an ill-tempered individual." The end of this poem was not much different from its beginning; He wrote:

"…But when I missed you Mohamed, I missed in you what I had hoped to have for ever."

Ahmad Ibn Souleiman also wrote poems about his ascetism and piety.

"I forsook the great and precious value of life and leave it for those who give it much importance. Thanks God, I forsook willingly a life of indulgence as death forsook me. I thank God for enabling me to keep away from the glamour of a material life, and I became disterested in riches. Had people understood my view, they would have become more insightful, and would have said, Ahmad is very pertinent."

*The picture shows one of the pages of the holy Koran written in gold on a parchment. It is one of the vestiges of the old library of Okhba Ben Nafaa Mosque in Kairwan. On this parchment were written some verses of the Surat: "AL KASSAS" (the stories)*

# The fall of the Aghlabites'state:

The Abbassides' kalifates became increasingly fearful of the Allaouis in Syria and of those who were associated with them of the Shiaa sect after the uprisings that took place among some of their chiefs in Medina and Bassra in Irak like Mohamed Ibn Maarouf known as the "chaste soul" and his brother. Finally, the Abassides got rid of the sectarianism on which they had previously founded their state; this resulted into the aggressive reaction of the Allaouins by causing disturbances in order to overthrow the Abasside state in the hegira year 169. In North Africa, Idriss Ibn Abdullah, of the Shiaa sect, went to Morocco disseminating the Shiaa doctrine in the form of a religion. He managed to rally the Berbers around him and they acknowledged him as a sovereign. He founded there (in Morocco) the Addarissa state (in accordance with his name, Idriss). The khalifa, Haroun Arrashid (in Irak), accordingly founded in Ifrikya, (Tunisia) the Aghlabites'state. He acted in the same way as someone who, seeing fire breaking into one part of his house separates this part from the rest of the house in order to save Ifrikya from the uprisings caused by the Shiaa sect in Morocco and in the Middle East.

Idrissi's missionionary work in Morocco was for the propagation of the Shiaa doctrine and for a planned Shiaa invasion of Morocco, especially that the Shiaa sect had established a particular order known as the missionary order. They sent their messsengers to all the Islamic continents east and west. Besides, they caused an insurrection that broke out in the Middle East after paving the way to it with the help of the "Karamita" (a tribe of

Berbers and Arabs in Morocco), an insurrection that shook terribly the Abbasides reign. This resulted into the rising of another Shiia group in Ifrikya (Tunisia) called the Fatimides. The cunning Shiite propagandist, Abu Abdullah Assanaani, paved the way for a rebellion. The historian, Abou Dinar, reminded us that Assanaani learned the secret message of the Fatimides from Ibn Houshib whom he had sent to Morocco to inquire into the state of things of the Shiaa in Morocco. Then he went to Mecca during the pilgrimage period and met with the "Koutama" kinsfolk in Morocco. He played the role of a scholar telling this Moroccan tribe about the virtues of the Prophet's household. He succeeded in his sheme. He made friends with the Koutama kinsfolk. They sympathised with him and asked him about his next destination. He pretended that he was heading for Egypt to pursue his studies. But they invited him to Morocco. He accepted the invitation without showing them his real intention. In the meantime, he inquired about their country and their

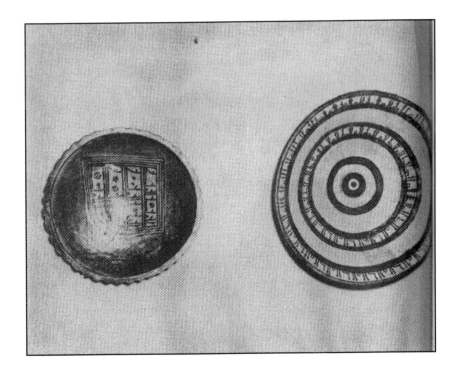

*An Aghlabite ceramic and mosaic found in an excavation in Rakkada.*

kinsfolk until he got a thorough knowledge of everything. When they reached Morocco, the Berbers beseeched him to stay with them. He became so famous that people came to see him from everywhere until his secret scheme was revealed and his news as a spy spread out throughout Morocco and Ifrikya. Ziadout Allah, the Aghlabite prince, sent a huge army to kill him and kill those who joined him among the Berber tribes. The two armies met near El Kef, in the north west of Tunisia. A bloody war broke out between the two armies. Unfortunately, Ziadatu Allah's army suffered many adversities and he finally lost the war. So he gathered what remained of his army, collected his assets and escaped to the Middle East. As for the propagandist, Abou Abdullah Assanaani, when he learned about the escape of Ziadout Allah to the Middle East, he gathered an army and invaded Kairwan. Once there, he reassured its inhabitants that they would live in total security under his reign. He rook over power, then returned to Morocco; he saved his master Ubaidallah Al Mahdi from his detention camp, the he returned to Ifrikya and settled in Rakadda in the outskirts of Kairwan. He took control of power and called himself the Commander of the Faithful. To him (Assanaani) was attributed the Ubaidia state.

The fall of the Aghlabites'state was due to many factors, such as the expulsion of a bigger part of the Arab army whose soldiers had setlled in Kairwan after its invasion although that army was considered the greatest support of the Arab power in Ifrikya. Besides, Ziadoutallah was an alcoholic who led a life of indulgence neglecting almost entirely the affairs of the state. Another factor that led to the weakening of the Aghlabites'state was that the Berbers were disappointed by the repugnant fanaticism of the Arabs denying the Berbers'efficient participation in the Islamic conquests; this explained why the Koutama tribes joined the Shiaa sects.

# The Ubaidi era (296-361 Hegir)

## I. The settlement of the Ubaidi state

This era did not last more than 65 years during which four of the Fatimide governors reigned successively, Abu Ubaidallah Al Mahdi, Abul Kassem and Ismaiel Al Mansur and Moez Lidin Allah Al Mansur Al Fatimi. But the sweeping uprisings which broke out during that period was a hindrance to the survival of the Ubaidia rule. Those uprisings caused Ifrikya to shake under the doctrinal conflicts between the Sunna and the Shiaa sects. This resulted into the persistence of spiteful antagonistic hostilities which were stifled now and then by the effect of oppression, but they broke out finally to give vent to tragic disasters.

Hardly did Ubaidullah Al Mahdi settle in Rakadda that he found himself in a dangerous position that caused fear and panic everywhere. On the one hand, the tribes of Koutama and their chiefs thought that they should have the upper hand as if Ifrikya were a Berber state because it was thanks to them that this state (the Ubaidia) triumphed and was empowered to govern in Ifrikya. But on the other hand, the Shiaa propagandist Abu Ubaidullah Assanaani, Al Mahdi's supporter became wary and discontent, his dubious consent portended a deceitful scheme. Besides, the people of Kairwan and Rakadda considered the Shiaa sect as polytheists and wishing that some calamity would befall them.

All these misgivings exasperated the kalifate Al Mahdi and made him use every means to consolidate his government in order to protect it from the danger of rebellions and unexpected uprisings. So he killed his propagandist Abu Ubaidullah and his brother Abul Abass. Then he wrote to the Shiaa sect in the Middle East what follows: "I hope you have been informed about the attitude of Abu Ubaidallah and his brother Abu Al Abass towards Islam. The devil made them sin and apostatize. So I purified their souls with the sward." Afterwards, he lavished a lot of money on the Shi'its and made them feudal lords after getting rid of some of their chiefs. His rule was full of terror. In fact, he made the people of Kairwan and Rakkada live in constant fear. He punished cruelly all those who stood against his doctrine. He chose among his royal guard thousands of Roman and black slaves to avoid being guarded by Arab soldiers.

Accordingly, Al Mahdi managed to silence all the antagonistic movements, but it was only a kind of quietude, so to speak, before the tempest. Al Mahdi sensed actually a latent danger from Kairwan, the birthplace of the Sunna sect. So he decided to leave it and started exploring the sea coasts of Ifrikya in search of a secure place where he could build a military base for his kingdom. He eventually reached a peninsula located between Soussa (in the center east) and Sfax (in the south east) which he chose as a place of settlement. He ordered buildings to be erected there. Then he called the place "Mahdia" in attribution to his name.

What he first built was a strong rampart to the west and a shipyard. When many buildings were erected in Mahdia, he moved to it in 308 of the Hegir and made it a base for the Ubaidia caliphate. He also built its well-known mosque and a palace for his successor, his son Abu Al Kassem Al Mahdi.

When his grandson Ismael Al Mansur took over, he returned to Kairwan and built in its outskirts a town called "Al Mansuria" which bears nowadays the name of "Sabra". Al Mansur made Al Mansuria a seat for the caliphate in 337. Then he transferred to it all the shops and worshops of Kairwan, and he embellished it with gardens and orchards.

*The main entrance of Mahdia Mosque edified by Ubaidullah Al Mahdi,
the founder of Mahdia in the early years of the fourth century.*

## II. The rebellion Of Sakeb Al Himar:

One of the most drastically violent rebellion that Ifrikya underwent
was that of Abi Yazid Mokhlod Bin Kaidad nicknamed "Saheb Al Himar",
that is the donkey's friend.

Ibnu Yazid grew up in Tozeur (south west of Tunisia) and abode by its
mosque teaching the children of the area the Holy Koran. He used to ride

a donkey and to wear woollen clothes summer and winter. He pretended to be pious and to be God-fearing. He claimed to be calling for truth, to be defending true religion and to be standing against the Shiaa heresy. All these deceitful means induced the Berbers to love him so much that he became popular and powerful. He sent his soldiers to Tunis who penetrated it deliberately. They abused the women there, killed the children, plundered its people, and demolished its mosques. They moved to Beja ( in the north west) and devastated it. Then they made for another town in the middle west called Fahs Ibn Salah near Zaghouan and they were defeated overwhelmingly there. The governor Al Kaem Bin Amrallah sent them a huge army and killed them ruthlessly. Four thousand were killed, five hundred were made prisoners and the rest of the army were chased away. But Abu Yazid Al Mokhled did not repent. He prepared another army and made another devastating assault this time on Kairwan. His army was estimated at one hundred thousand between cavalry and infantry. They desecrated and killed their enemy. They threatened to exterminate the Kairwan people if "they failed to go with him (Yazid) on Jihad. He told them that their blood and their properties would be permissible. Many people were scared to death and reluctantly joined him. He sent his troops to all Ifrikyan cities and sea ports plundering shops and getting hold of weapons. After invading Kairwan, they marched on Soussa and beseiged it. Then they went to Mahdia, beseiged it firmly for so long that livelihood became very expensive and scarce, so people began to starve and epidemics and calamities spread out.

In the meantime, Al Kaem Bi Amr Allah died and his son Al Mansur took over. He kept secret his father's death. He made use of his state's power in order to kill Abu Yazid, the dictator, and exterminate his army. He scared Koutama's tribes to war and went himself on war with them. He defeated Yazid, wounding him badly, then he confined him in a cage and ordered him to be shown around in Kairwan. After that, he took him to Mahdia and crucified him on its main gate; that was in 336. Yazid's son rebelled against the hideous killing of his father and wanted to avenge him. Al Mansur sent him a group of his soldiers and they killed him.

These disturbances which afflicted Ifrikya disastrously by devastating it, disquietening its people and disconcerting its kings for long periods was a hindrance to its development. Many of its installations which stood for a highly civilized and urbanized state were uprooted and eradicated. The blame for all these disasters was to be put on the Berbers, the first descendents of Ifrikya, whose naivety was a favorable playground for propagandists and dissenters to distabilize Ifrikya. The historian Yakhut, described the Berbers "as being very submissive to the advocators of perversity, and to those who encouraged unrest and bloodshed. Many a leader among the propagandists and dissenters claimed he was the promised Messiah and they believed him credulously, embracing his doctrine. The dissenters had such a great influence on them so that after Islam, they adopted thoughtlessly their doctrine."

### III. The transfer of the caliphate to Egypt

Much did Abu Ubaidullah try to convince the people of Ifrikya by reasoning and by sending them the scholars of the Shiaa sect to persuade them to adopt their ideolgy, but it was to no avail. So he resorted to force and bloodshed. The Kairwan people stuck to their doctrine, the Sunna doctrine, because they saw in the Shiaa doctrine a renunciation of religion. The historian, Abu Naji, pointed out in his book, "Maalem Al Imaan" (the characteristic feature of faith) to the fact that when Ubaidullah reigned over Kairwan, the Shiaa scholars did their utmost to change the natives' belief by compelling them to opt for the Shiaa ideology through discussion and the exchange of ideas, then through controversial debate, but they were unsuccessful. The king killed two disciples of Imam Sehnun. The people were scared. They resorted to a scholar and advocator of Sunna ideology named Essaied Ibnu Mohamed Al Ghassani known as "Ibnul Haddad". He was one of the most discerning jurists and he accepted to defend their cause. He declared, "I'm nearing ninety and I don't care whether I live or die. It's quite obvious that the dissenter proves to be the best killer. ( meaning the Shiaa fighter) So fighting for religion is a must if one wants God's forgiveness."

This shows that the debates that took place between the "Sunna" and the "Shiaa" often made the Sunnits victims of persecution and torture. One can give the example of a Sunnist scholar called Bakir Mohamed Ibnu Labbad who refused to comply with the Shiaa doctrine and continued to oppose to their arguments. He was jailed for life until he died in prison in 333. Another example is that of Ibnul Haddad who bore a bitter enmity to the Shiaa sect and their ideology. One day in a meeting, he spoke in favor of the Sunna doctrine. He ventured into a convincing debate with Abu Mussa, a Shiite; the latter lost his temper and was about to stab him if Abu Abdullah, another Shiite, did not hold him back. Then he turned to Ibnul Haddad and said: " Do not anger this scholar because twelve thousand swards will avenge his anger." Ibnul Haddad replied: " As for me, my anger will cause God's anger, God the Almighty who annihilated the people of Aad and Thamud and many other tyrannical people centuries ago within a short time." (Those people were quoted in the Holy Koran because they were oppressive and atheists)

The reign of Al Mahdi ended. Then Al Kaem took over. Then came the reign of Al Mansur. The Ubaidia army continued to march on the Maghreb, but to no avail because it proved to be impossible to impose on Al Mahdi and his successors their rule. So people broke away with Al Mahdis'kings and lived isolated from them. This critical situation proved to be an incentive for Moez Allah Al Fatimi to leave Ifrikya and go to Egypt. Another incentive was the disorderly political situation that Egypt endured, especially after the death of her king Kafur Al Akhshidi, let not speak of the dashing bravery and heroism that characterized "Jaafar Assiklli," who was the upper arm of the dead king. Assikilli marched with his army across Morocco, seized Fes ( A Moroccan town conquered by the Aghlabites) and killed ruthlessly those who stood on his way.

Some historians justified the removal of the Ubaidia caliphate to Egypt by the fact that the country, Egypt, was poor and shffered from a shortage of resources to carry out the affairs of a big country whose people were inclined to lead a life of opulance, comfort and pleasure. Other historians were not in favor of this idea. The great Tunisian historian Ibnu Khaldun stated that, "when Jaouhar Assikilli, the commander of the Ubaidia army set off from Kairwan to Egypt, he brought with him enough money to pay the soldiers and to provide for the livelihood of the military expedition, and no country has ever reached the miserable condition that Egypt undewent." When Jaouhar marched on Egypt, he did not find the least resistance from Al Akhshidi's army which took to flight. Then he planned another city close to Egypt which he called "the Moazia Cairo".

In the year 361, Al Moez left Al Mansuria in a gloriously unprecendented procession. He entrusted the principality of Ifrikya to Abi Al Fattouh Balkia Ben Ziri from the Berber Sanhaja tribe as an acknowledgement to him and to his father for their august services in support of the Ubaidia state.

Al Moez strongly advised Balkia to take into consideration three recommendations while reigning. First, he must not attack the Berbers or seize their properties. Second, he must not levy taxes on peasants. Third, he must not delegate the reign to any of his household so that they will not think that they are more entitled for the reign than the others.

Al Moez appointed also Hassan Ibnu Ali governor of Sicily because he did not want Balkia to lay his hands on it. He took this precautionary measure in order not to leave the domination of the sea get out of his grip. Finally, he appointed Abdullah Ibnu Yakhlaf Al kutami governor of Tripoli in Libya.

Commenting on the removal of the caliphate to Egypt, Ibn Khaldun wrote: "That was the last epoch of the Arabs'reign on Ifrikya. In fact, Koutama (a Berber) was given control of everything; after him came the turn of the Berbers of Morocco. Therefore, the Arabs and their reign on Ifrikya had gone with the wind."

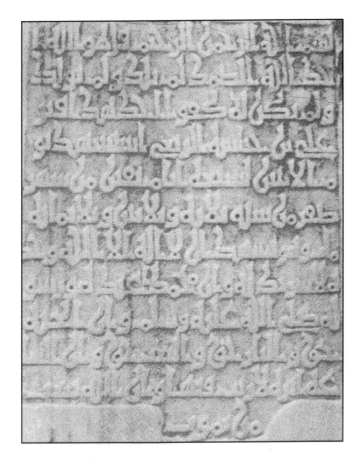

*This is a tombstone on which was written:*

The buried man died in the same year as Saheb Al Himar assaulted on Kairwan. On this tombstone is engraved the following:

In the name of God, the Most Gracious, the Most Merciful, along with some short surats from the Holy Koran.

This is the tombstone of Ali Ibnu Habassa Arrbii. Died on Monday, seven days before the end of Safar (second month of the Hegir ) in 333.

He died testifying that God the One Has no partner and that Mohamed is His Slave and His Messenger, Peace Be Upon Him, and that Paradise is truth, that Hell is truth, that Resurrection is truth, that Doomsday is truth, and that God Resurrects the dead.

## IV. The scholastic movement in the Ubaidi era

When the Ubaidi state extended its dominion over Ifrikya, the Shiaa propagandists were there to disseminate their doctrine backing it up with whatever evidence and argument they could provide. The state supported and protected them from the Sunnits' diatribe and strong disapproval. Kairwan boasted at that time of the great number of Sunnit scholars who were versed in theological matters. Neither threats nor menace deterred them from speaking out their ideas. Not only did they take a negative stance towards the Shi'ite propagandist campaign which started to have an effective impact on the Berbers, but they also rebuffed their opponents and bravely challenged their ideology by criticizing them bitterly and accusing them of apostasy in spite of the ruthless and abusive persecussions they underwent.

Nevertheless, the controversial arguments and contests between the two sects gave birth to a sharp-witted theological and scholastic movement which urged people on both sides to write hundreds of books. For example the Shi'ite theologians coined so-to speak a heretic ideology according to which the Imams originating from Fatima's kinsfolk were sinless and pure. Besides, the Shiaa Imams invoked after Friday sermons and prayers not only the Prophet Mohamed (PUB), but also his cousin Ali, his daughter Fatima, his grandchildren, Ali's sons Al Hassan and Al Houssain. They also lauded the Prophet's Companions, the orthodox caliphates and the Commander of the Faithful's father, Imam Al Mahdi.

The contemporay Tunisian historian Ibnu Abi Addhiaf narrated that the king Ubaidullah Al Mahdi gathered in his palace in Rakadda the Shiaa Imams and ordered them to add in their invocations on Friday prayers and on Aids ( Moslem Feasts) the following invocation:

"God 's blessing and peace be upon thy slave and custodian, the guardian of thy slaves in thy land, Abi Mohamed Ubaidullah Al Mahdi Billah, the Commander of the Faithful, the same as Thou Blest and Prayed on his fathers, the Mahdi Orthodox, Thy caliphs whose rule was just and right. God Almighty, Thou selected him to be governor and caliph and made him sinless and loyal, May Thou make him triumph over Thy sinful foes. Assist him in the conquest of all the globe, east and west. Be for him a support against his pervert apostates. God, Thou art the Revealer of Truth."

In the opinion of the Shiaa sect, religion has apparent and hidden interpretations. Its texts, the Holy Koran and the Prophet's Hadith, have both explicit and implicit meanings. According to them, prophets are the legislators of religious law. Like politicians, they were sent to the masses, while philosophers and thinkers were sent to the wizards. Therefore, the Shiaa sect divided people into two classes: the laymen and the intellectuals and philosophers. Besides, they held meetings special for the masses and meetings special for the particulars, that is the intellect.

It was narrated that Al Moez Al Fatimi wrote to the Shiaa propagandists what follows:

"Keep secret the affairs of the state. Do not reveal them to the masses, but discuss them with the elite. Do not reveal to the commons all that belittles their minds because they cannot grasp the incomprehensible. Do not trust those who do not deserve to be trustworthy. Do not sow but a fertile land, and do not grow in your field but fruitful plants." (meaning the masses and the elite).

Malek's doctrinal books and concepts seemed quite restricted and restrained in comparison to the Shiaa's doctrinal concepts. Actually, Malek's doctrine was characterized by its conformity to the Koran and to the Prophet's Hadith. Malek did his best to avoid interpretations. For him the transcription of the Koran or Hadith should be prior to their interpretation. The same could be said about the use of reason in judgment and verdicts. In other words, the scholar and jurist should always rely on what exists in the Book and the Prophet's Hdith and not on reasoning. So Malek's doctrinal concepts were far from the Shiaa's complex ideolgy based on strange legislations and far-fetched and ambigious interpretations.

So, the gap separating the Kairwan scholars and jurists, who took on themselves to emulate Malik's conduct and principles of life, from the Shiaa scholars was wide . The Shiaa scholars appeared under different lights. Besides, they talked to every walk of people the language they could understand. They resorted to the rational in their dealings. They justified every endeavor they excercised to the satisfaction and obedience of kings and princes and also to the dissemination of the Shiaa doctrine.

What is noticeable is that the Shiaa did not find in Ifrikya the favorable opportunity to propagate and develop their doctrine, and this is because most of the Kairwan scholars were opposed to their ideology considering it as heretic. Nevertheless, a few Kairwan scholars complied with the Shiaa. They adopted their doctrine and familiarized with it. They even excelled the Shi'ite scholars and propagandists in the dessimination of the Shiaa doctrine. They managed to write proficiently lots of books about the precepts of the Shiaa doctrine. When Al Moez moved to Cairo, they accompanied his convoy. One of the most famous converts to the Shiaa was:

## 1.Ubaidullah Ibnul Hassan Al Kairwani.

He was known to be the adept of the Ismailia philosophy. He wrote to one of the advocators of this philosophy the following: "if you come across a philosopher, stick to him and befriend him because we are entirely dependent on philosophers"

## 2.Annumaan Ibnu Mohamed Ibnu Hayoun:

He was at first a Sunnit and more precisely a Maliki, then he converted overnight into the doctrine of the Imamia, according to which the Imam was the only representative of God on earth and a competent authority to the commons. Annumaan was appointed a magistrate in Egypt, then his descendants succeeded him consequently for a long period of time during the Fatimides' rule. In fact, the Nomaan dynasty succeeded in their mission after converting into Shi'ites, such as Mohamed Annoumaan and his son Abdel Aziz. Like his father, Abdel Aziz was versed in the science of Imamia.

### 3. Ibnu Kuthair:

A Sunnit historian, Hadith narrator and Koran interpreter, wrote a book about the Shiaa dogma entitled "The greatest Edict and the most valuable Law". Abu Bakr Al Balkani, a Sunnite scholar replied in a book entitled: "Nothing is greater and more glorious than God Almighty."

By and large, the scholastic movement enlived the Ubaidi era thanks to the development of dialectics and discourse. Then came the renewal of the "House of Wisdom" (Baitul Hikma) which had continued to fulfill its duty since its creation by the Aghlabites until it was transferred from Kairwan to Cairo in Egypt by the Fatimides who carried along with it its legacy, that is its books which had been first arrayed in Kairwan's "House of Wisdom" . At the same time many scholars left Kairwan and went to Cairo.

Thousands of books in different fields of knowledge were removed from the libraries of Kairwan to Cairo or to the palace of the Fatimide caliphate, Al Aziz Ibnul Moez Lidin Allah Al Fatimi. Nevertheless, the radiance of those transferred books had for many years such a great impact on the development of the scholastic and literary activities on Ifrikya, particularly in the Sanhaji era.

As for the ancient library which came into being in the Aghlabites' era, and installed in one of the rooms of Okhba Mosque in Kairwan, it was ignored entirely by the Fatimides. They did not remove it to Cairo because it contained only ornated books of the Holy Koran and the Prophet's Hadith along with a few books of Malek's jurisprudence.

## V. A scholastic debate

Mohamed Ibnul Hareth narrated in his book "Classes of Ifrikya's scholars"about the debates held between the Shiaa propagandists and the Maliki scholars. During a competing meeting between Abu Othman Ibnu Saiid Ibnul Haddad and Abul Abass Al Makhdun Ashii, during which a comparison was made between, the prophet Moses and his brother Harun, and Ali ( the Prophet's companion and cousin) and his sons Al Hussin and Al Hussain. According to Abu Othman (a sunnit), Harun was an authority and an evidence of Moses'existence, but Ali was not an evidence of Mohamed's existence. He was not an authority either. He was only his minister, and all the Prophets' companions were his ministers. For Abul Abass (a Shi'it) Ali was like Harun to Moses. He came just after the Prophet Mohamed both in rank and esteem, that is, Ali was superior to the other Prophet's companions.

## VI. The most renouned scholars and jurists:

### 1. Abdullah Ibnu Zaed Annafzaoui:

He was born in Kairwan in 310 of the Hegir and grew up in quest of knwoledge. He was versed in theology besides his being intelligent and insightful enough to reply questions set by some prejudiced and whimsical people, particularly among the Shiaa scholars. He became so renouned thanks to his broad knowledge that he was nicknamed "Malek junior". Scholars from every corner of the Islamic world immigrated to Kairwan to learn from him. His most well-known book is "The Message" (Arrissala). He sent a copy to Abi Bakr Al Abhari, a Maliki scholar in Baghdad who commended it and publicized it among the masses and the learned men. The book was so successful that it was sold out within a short time and its writer earned lavish royalties from it.

Annafzaoui wrote other books like "The Book of Anecdotes", "What is to be annexed to the law Codes" and "A Concise book of the law Codes."

Annafzaoui was veory generous towards the poor and spendthrift with the foreign students who travelled to Kairwan to pursue their theological studies. He died and was buried in Kouraish graveyard in Kairwan.

This is one of his poems in which he eligized his scholar and teacher Abu Bakr Ibnu Mohamed Allabed persecuted by the Fatimides because he refuted their ideology. They threw him in prison and was kept prisoner until he died. This is a concise paraphrase of his eligy:

" I longed for the sight of a man who had disappeared from existence, but his remembrance is deeply engraved in my mind and heart. I grieved for a dead man who sacrified his life for the rivival of Islam and the Sunna of the Prophet"(PUB)

*The ruins of a room in one of the Ubaidia palaces in Mansura, Kairwan.*

## VII. The literary movement:

The Ubaidia state was founded on the basis of propaganda and propagandists. Poetry coud be compared then to the newspapers and magazines nowadays. The poets were lucky enough to find the Ubaidia kings and princes so lavish that they bestowed on them an abundance of gifts and money in exchange for lauding them and praising their doctrine in scores of eulogizing poems. The leading poet known for his extravagant eulogies was a Moroccan who went by the name of Ibnul Hani.

### 1. Ibnul Hani:

He eulogized the Fatimide king Al Moez so profusely that the latter lavished on him valueless gifts and a lot of money. It was rumored that when Ibnul Hani eulogized him in an epic poem, he gave him six thousand dinars and he ordered that a palace worth six other thousand dinars should be built for him. These are some extracts of this eulogizing poem.

"My Lord, your will and God's will are alike. Will you rule and you are undoubtedly the Mighty One. You are like Prophet Mohamed, and your supporters are like the Prophet's Companions. You are the One whom Christian bishops heralded of your Advent in their Books."

The Ubaidia poetry was concerned mainly with the dissemination of the Shiaa doctrine, the lauding of the Prophet's family and their enhancing the Shiaa's kinship to the level of the Prophet's family. This is what one of the Fatimides' poets wrote:

"Sons of Fatima (the Prophet's daughter), we have no refuge to take during our Resurrection but in you. You are the Protectors and the Saviours. You are God's well-beloved slaves and His faithful descendants on earth. You are entitled to be God's prophets, messengers, leaders to the right guidance and sinless conduct. Whenever people conjure up God's noblest creatures, they point out to you. If ever you touch a rock, streams and rivers will gush out and flow forth."

Another kind of the Shiaa poetry is sentimental and emotional.The Shiaa poetry excelled by far the Sunnit's because it was freed from the shackles of religion which had generally prevailed on Ifrikyan poetry since the Aghlabites'era. Strict religion had in fact hindered Sunnit poets to be jocular, emotional and creative as Shi'it poets were. Their poetry was distinguished by being tender, warm-hearted, outstandingly imaginative and beautifully written, especially erotic poetry. This is an extract from Ibnul Hani's erotic poetry. This is a love poem in which Ibnul Hani was courting a beautiful female dancer:

"Shall your beautiful eyes or your nice songs be our courting place? Shall I meet you in the slumbering valley or in the lovers'valley? They deprived you of slumber and they walked away surruptitiously. Should they they fall upon the specter of a night comer, they would suspect you. They left you entranced without being drunk. When your swaying body twisted, they accused you believing that the kohl on your eyelids an adornment.But by God, they did not darken your eyes with their hands."

## 2. Tamim Abi Hanifa Annomaan Al Kairwani:

He was at first one of the most famous Maliki scholars, then he converted to Shiaa doctrine. He studied philosophy, logic and dialectics. He was appointed governor of Egypt during the reign of Al Moez and his son Al Aziz. When he wrote poetry, he dared mentioning what the Sunnits considered as sinful in erotic poetry. In fact, he combined what is serious with the humorous in solemn situations when one should, according to the Sunnites, be submissive to God and should praise only God. This is one of Tamimi's erotic poems:

"Many a beautiful female did I encounter in Arafat (A mountain near Mecca where pilgrims spend a whole night praying and invoking God during pilgrimage). They deprived me of my virtues because I kept feasting my eyes and admiring their fascinating beauty.They violated my holiness. They inflamed my heart and boiled my impatience when they made for the place of "embers" (this is one of the Haj rituals when pilgrims have to pelt the Devil with seven stones).

Many poets lived at that time in Al Moez Al Fatimi's palace in Mahdia, such as Ali Ibnu Al Ayadi Attounissi, Ali Abdullah Attounissi and others. The Moroccan poet Ibnul Hani boasted of his poetry and belittled and made fun of those poets.

Among the renouned Kairwan literary men was Abul Arab Tamimi, the writer of "A Classification of Ifrikya's Scholars." He was also the writer of "The Virtues of Malik Ibnu Anass". The Ubaidi kings imprisoned him because he attacked the Shiaa doctrine.Among the most prestigious Kairwan poets, one can mention

### 3.Abul Kassem Al Fazzari:

This is a paraphrase of a poem in which he lauded the town of Kairwan.

"Will Kairwan and its people be equalled when one starts to laud them? Kairwan is a town of knowledge, clemency, true Islam, gratitude and genrosity. The Irak of Ishaam is Baghdad, but Kairwan whose relation with Baghdad is very intimate, is Baghdad of the west."

### 4.Mohamed Ibnu Hani Al Azdi:

His father Hani was a poet, too. He lived in a village in the outskirts of Mahdia, then he moved to Andalusia, and there was born his son Mohamed in 326 in Seville and was brought up there. Mohamed was an inborn poet.Then he became a famous philosopher. The Andalusians who were Sunnits accused him of atheism and apostasy. The prince of Seville then advised him to leave the town for fear of being killed. So he left for Ifrikya at the age of 27. When Al Moez Al Fatimi heard of him, he received him hospitably. Therefore, he started writing poems eulogizing and glorifying the generous king. When Al Moez moved to Cairo, Ibnu Hani joined him. One day, a wealthy Libyan man invited him to his palace and treated him to generous banquets. Ibnu Hani stayed in his palace for a few days during which he went to salons of amusement and wine in Tripoli. It was told that Ibnu Hani left one night the salon intoxicated. He was found lying dead on the road. It was in 336 of the Hegir and he was then 36 of age.

His poetry was characterized by an exaggerated eulogy. The blind Arab poet of the time Al Maarri commented on his poetry and said: "The words of Ibnu Hani's poetry are like a mill grinding horns." In fact, Ibnu Hani used rattling and ringing words in his poems, and this is in imitation of Al Mutanabbi, a middle eastern poet of the time who was contemporary to Ibnu Hani. The praising poems that Ibnu Hani wrote to eulogize Al Moez Al Fatimi could be compared to Al Motanabbi's praising poems that he wrote in praise of the Syrian King nicknamed "Saifu Addouala" (The sward of the state) or the Egyptian king, Kafur Al Ehkshidi. In these poems, Al Moutanabbi praised Saifu Addaoula's ideology and good deeds. He also commended his adventurous and heroic assaults when he ventured into wars against his apostatic enemies.

In comparison to Al Moutanabbi's poetry,this is a poem in which Ibnu Hani lauded Al Moez Al Fatimi. He started the poem with wooing his lover, then he moved to bidding the king farewell:

"They (female singers) attended their lovers'funeral ceremonies wearing mourning dresses and darkening their eyes( with kohl) in sorrow. They shed their affectionate tears upon parting so much so that we were infatuated with them on a sad parting day."

In a poem in which Ibnu Hani lauded Jaouhari Issikilli, describing his departure from Ifrikya accompanied by his battalion of cavalry men. It was when Jaouhar was ordered by Al Moez to leave Kairwan for the conquest of Egypt:

"He (meaning Jaouhar) was leading a battalion of dashing cavalry men ; the spectacle was more awsome than Doomsday. I was so confused by this terrific sight that I knew not how to bid farewell or to greet him. The motionless mountains looked as if marching in his company, prostrating and bowing at the rustle of his passing horsemen."

*The ruins of one of the Ubaidis' castle in Sabra, Al Mansura (the outskirts of Kairwan) in the 4ᵗʰC*

# The Sanhaji era

## I. The Sanhaji princes:

### 1. Youssef Balkin:

When Al Moez Lidin Allah Al Fatimi decided to move away to Egypt, he chose one of Ziri Ibnu Manad's sons, Youssef Balkin, to be his successor in Ifrikya. He made Youssef Balkin Ibnu Ziri Ibnu Manad a caliphate on Ifrikya. This man was of Berber origin, from the Sanhaja tribe which proclaimed to be a supporter of the Shiaa doctrine and swore its allegiance to the Ubaidia caliphates. The Sanhajia tribe proved to be overwhelmingly destructive of all those who rebelled against them.

Ziri, for example, was of a dashing bravery. He was also vehemently powerful. He fought boldly Saheb Al Himar's uprisings and succeeded to defeat him. He did the same with the rebellious Zinata tribes which bore an old grudge against the Sanhajis and waged many wars against them. Had it been the bravery of Ziri and the great courage of his army, Jaouhar Assikilli would have never been able to crush the Zanati rebellion in Morocco or the conquest of Fes city in Morocco. It was for all these reasons that the Fatimid caliphate installed the Sanhaji household on the reign of Ifrikya.

After bidding Al Moez farewell by escorting him along with his army to Egypt, Youssef Balkin returned and stayed two months in Al Mansuria in order to appoint governors over the different Ifrikyan towns. Soon after, he went back to Ashir, the capital of Sanhaja in Algeria, to repress the successive uprisings that Zanata tribes trigged off all over Morocco. He managed finally to fight so ruthlessly the dissenters that he became powerful, awed and revered by everyone. He chose Ashir to be the seat of his reign. The city of Ashir had been built by his father Ziri in the tribal mountains of Algeria. Ziri settled in Ashir to be constantly watching the Zanata tribes which swore to go on continuous hostile wars against the Sanhaja tribes.

## 2. Prince Al Mansur:

Youssef edified three cities in Algeria, Meliana, Algiers and Media. When he died, his son "Al Mansur" took over and settled in Ashir. The historian Ibnul Athir narrated that scholars, jurists and the elite came from Kairwan to offer Al Mansur their condolences and congratulated him for taking over the reign. He received them warmly and told them: "My father and my grandfather treated you with vehement fierceness, but I am going to treat you kindly." Then he started criticizing severely the Egyptian caliphate, claiming that the caliphate could not dethrone him by a simple letter stating that "he is not the one to be throned or dethroned by a simple letter." Al Aziz Al Fatimi, the Egyptian governor might have been informed about Al Mansur's insulting words. He tried to dethrone him by force, but when he failed, he offered him many gifts. Al Mansur sent him gifts in exchange. This is how Al Mansur reconciled with his opponents when he failed to fight them and triumph over them. He attracted them to him by shutting his eyes over their mistakes and tried to be clement and tolerated their mistakes.

Another example of Al Mansur's cunning and tricky policy was when he found out that the peasants were complaining of being overtaxed, he deducted their taxable income. This affected leniency had a positive impact on his success as a good ruler. Al Mansur died in 386. he was succeeded by his eldest son, Badis

### 3. Prince Al Moez Ibnu Badis:

Badis was enthroned in Mahdia in a magificent parade. But he was then too young to reign. Because of his young age, he was disdained and disrespected by Zanata's princes who rebelled against him in order to dethrone him. His uncle Hamada sent him a huge army which destabilized his enemies and defeated them at the end. When he gained the war, Hamada built for himself a stately tower. He used it as a base during his reign; this tower remained standing after him for his children and grandchildren.

The Sanhaji state was split into two parts, a state in the east of Ifrikya with its capital Kairwan, and a state in the west with its seat, Hamada's tower. However, this partition did not have a serious effect on the entity of the Sanhaji rule or power as was the case of partitions that led sometimes to the disappearance of the reigning state. Besides, Badisis'reigning period was full of bloody wars and mutinies that urged Badis to leave Mahdia for sometime and go on frequent visits to Kairwan. One day he heard that Ziri Ben Attia Azzanati left Morocco for Ashir city in Algeria. He prepared a huge army to fight him. The two antagonistic armies encountered near Thirit in Algeria and a raging war broke out ending with Badisis' army's defeat. His army was driven away and his soldiers were scattered. Then Ziri seized all the booty from weapons, furniture and money.

When Badis was told about his army's defeat, he left Rakkada and made for Ashir in Algeria heading a huge army. This time, victory was on his side. He fought ruthlessly Ziri's army, so that when Ziri felt he was about to be vanquished, he retreated to Morocco. But the war did not end; it continued for so long between Badis and his enemies the Zanatis until Badis was killed in Mahdia which was then the capital of Ifrikya. After his death, his son Al Moez succeeded him in 406, and he was still nine. His father's uncle Hamad coveted for the reign of Ifrikya. He did his utmost to usurp the reign from his nephew by capturing the second half of Ifrikya, but when he failed he withdrew back to his fortress in Algeria. When Al

Moez became mature, he showed a great ability in handling judiciously the affairs of the state; The Fatimide caliphate conferred upon him the name of "The Honor of the State."Al Moez was also a gifted poet, cognizant of musical tunes and rhythm, in addition to his being generous, lenient and courageous.

The historian Ibnul Athir narrated that when Hamad tried to beseige some areas that belonged to Al Moez and failed he ran away, he asked Al Moez's forgiveness which was granted to him. Al Moez went so far as to ennoble him and satisfy his wish by marrying his daughter with his son Abdullah Ibnu Hamad. Al Moez's noble character enabled him to gain other Islamic courteous manners, which made the people gather around him and felt secure during his reign Unfortunately, the Fatimid caliphate in Egypt felt envious of Al Moez's successful policy because it made him popular and well- beloved. What the Fatimid caliphate wanted was a policy that did not leave the country in peace and calm. So he entrusted secretly a Berber tribe with sowing trouble and unrest in the country in order to weaken the sovereign and his government.

As a matter of fact, the Egyptian caliphate's envy and criminal intention schemed for the coming back of the Shi'its' sedition and their hostile rancor against the Sunnits. This resulted into bloody wars which ended with the death of thousands of innocents on both sides. When the situation in Ifrikya became critical, Al Moez saw it was high time he broke his relations with the Fatimids in Egypt. When the Egyptian caliphate AL Montassar was informed of this rupture, he decided to machinate against the Ifrikyan king Al Moez. He consulted his minister Al Hassan Al Yazouri who advised him to send an army of the frustrated tribes of the Upper Egypt, like Banu Hilal, Bani Salim, Riah and Zoghba, to Ifrikya to create havoc by making a savage assault on this continent. First, they marched on Kairwan like destructive hordes of locusts destroying and plundering whatever came on their way. Their attack was so violent and devastating that the Sanhaji army could not push them back in spite of its huge number. When Al Moez felt that they were going to lose the battle, he advised the people of Kairwan to leave their town and go with him to Mahdia. That was in 449. He deserted Kairwan and went to live with his son who was reigning over there. He stayed in Mahdia until he died in 453. After his death, his offspring took over.

The savage invasion that the bedouins of Upper Egypt made on Ifrikya in general and on Kairwan in particular was like an omen of the weakening of the Sanhaji reign and a forerunner of the end of the golden age in Kairwan and Ifrikya.

In fact, after that destructive assault, the Ifrikyan continent was torn into small principalities and shared between many sects and between the bedouin leaders of the Egyptian invaders so that the Sanhaji rulers had nothing left for them but a portion of land lying between Soussa (in the center east) and Gabes. (in the south east)

In the meantime, when the internal insurrections increased, the Normans invaded Sicily subjugating the Muslims living there to convert to Christianity or to pay high taxes. Captain Rajar of Sicily invaded Tripoli in Libya, Mahdia in Tunisia and most of the coastal cities in Ifrikya. It was Abdel Moomen Ibnu Ali Zanati who came from Morocco and freed Ifrikya from the grip of the Christians in 555 of the hegi, which corresponds to 1230 of the Christian date.

*The kings' prayer hall in Okhba Mosque*

A carved wooden fence that separates the kings' prayer hall from the rest of the mosque. At the top is engraved the following: "In the name of God the Merciful, the Gracious. Peace be upon Prophet Mohamed, his household and companions. This is what caliphate Abu Tamim Al Moez Ben Badis ordered to be done,etc…"

## II. The calamity that befell Kairwan:

As a rule, the Sunna doctrine was deeply rooted in Ifrikya, and in Kairwan in particular.This is due to the fact that it was well propagated by the Kairwan scholars so that it did not disappear easily as the Sunnit enemies thought it would be replaced easily by the Shiaa doctrine. In view of the Sunnits, the Shiaa doctrine was definitly apostatic and atheistic. So they took it for granted that fighting this doctrine was absolutely their duty because its persistance could lead to heresy and misguidance. Besides, if the Sunnit advocators were pitilessly persecuted in the Ubaidia era for the sake of true Islam and its protection from unbelievers. While supporting religion, they tried to disentangle themselves from any political or personal interests.

When the Sanhaji prince Balkin felt that the Sunnits'opposition to his affected support of the Shiaa sect started to turn against him, he pretended to sympathize with the Sunnits, but to be true, Balkin was neither Sunnit nor Shi'it.

The modern Egyptian historian Hussain Moeness put it, "Balkin was a cunning politician who searched for the best way to keep his seat safe." Therefore, when the Sunnits assailed the Shi'its, he was afraid to be dethroned by the Fatimid caliphate,so he struck hard at the Sunnits repressing uprisings that were about to break out, which resulted into the victimization of many Sunnit innocent people.

In the reign of Al Mansur Assanhaji, the Sunnits attacked the principality establishment and destroyed it. They launched an assault on the Shi'its when praying in their mosques. Al Mansur became sure that he was unable to impose his authority on the people of Ifrikya any more unless he sided cautiously and warily with the Sunnits, which he did.

When Al Moez Ibnu Badis took over, he noticed that most of the people were inclined towards the Sunna doctrine. So he broke abruptly with the Fatimid caliphate in Egypt and gave free rein to the Sunnits to do whatever they wanted with the Shi'its. So they started to burn, kill and plunder savagely whatever and whoever of the Shi'its came on their way. It was told that they killed about three thousand Shi'its in Kiarwan only. When the Fatimid caliphate learned about the tragic havoc the Sunnits made, he gave free rein to the Bedouin tribes of Upper Egypt to assault on Ifrikya and do whatever they wanted. When those savage Bedouins penetrated Kairwan, they devastated it and made havoc of every nook and corner, shouting out of anger and revenge, "This is Kairwan, here it is!" while destroying everything that came upon their way.

Kairwan was ruthlessly ravaged. Most of its establishments, institutions and mosques were destroyed in such a way that it plunged in total darkness and desolation. The scholastic and literary gatherings were disrupted. Business slumped. Kairwan suffered such a strong blow that it became unable to take off anew as Tunis did.

This horrid and tragic disaster that befell Kairwan inflamed the genius of many Kairwan poets who wrote eligies and eligies crying over a lost Paradise. This is f a part of an eligic poem written by Ibnu Rashik:

"The prestigious Okhba Mosque entirely devastated lay in deep darkness. This is the most tragic calamity that befell our dear Kairwan whose dreary sadness will be everlasting.Would the nights that have led Kairwan to perdition embrace her affectionately again so that Kairwan might have its golden past of the olden days restore to her?"

Another famous poet, Abil Hassan Al Houssari, eligized Kairwan in these lines:

"Would the enemies gloat at her (Kairwan) misfortuned fall? The sun does not eclipse but once in a while. He who Holds life tight in his grip, then Frees it (God) will either willingly annihilate Kairwan or preserve it.

Would Kairwan be restored to us? Would Sabra, Al Moalla and the ramparts be restored? When night falls, I feel depressed and saddened. I start heaving sorrowful sighs followed by moans and wails for the loss of Kairwan."

Thus Kairwan lived for ages in a gloomy stupor and forgetfulness. When the famous adventurer and explorer, Al Abdari visited Kairwan in the 7th.c of the Hegir. He wrote:

"When I arrived in Kairwan, I tried to find a scholar worthy of this name, but I found none except one who bore the name of "Addabegh". This means that even a feeble glow of science and knowledge disappeared almost entirely from Kairwan.

*A plate which dates back to the Sanhaji era*
*found near a barrack in Kairwan*

*A piece of painted pottery covering a wall in one
of the Ubaidia palaces in Sabra.*

### III. The Sanhaji policy:

It is to be remarked that the relationship between the Sanhaji princes and the Egyptian Fatimid caliphates was rather formal. The Fatimid caliphates' duty was to decree the appointment and honor the Sanhaji princes, but they did not meddle with the management of the state affairs or the appointment of civil servants because their objective was to show to be still authoritative, supreme and dominating, although that domination was merely theoritical and formal. This reminds us of the Ottoman supremacy in North Africa in the 18th and 19[th]c.

The supremacy of the Ottomans in North Africa in the nineteenth century for example was only formal and apparent. It was shown for propagation on pulpits after Friday prayers to claim a faked victory and a bygone power that the "Turkish Sultan is still a powerful sovereign enjoying supremacy over the two lands and the two seas." (meaning the east and the west)

In addition to their formal and apparent relationship, the Fatimid caliphates and the Sanhaji princes used to exchange presents. For example, although the Sanhaji prince Al Moez Ibnu Badis depreciated the caliphate Al Montasar Al Fatimi, he used to offer him many presents.

The contemporary Tunisian historian Abouddhiaf narrated that Al Moez Ibnu Badis stood on the side of the Sunnits ignoring the Fatimid caliphate as a means of defiance. However, he feared his minister, the wily Abil Hassan. He wrote to him loving letters as if he were his bosom friend. The minister ultimately perceived the prince's ill-intention.One day that vizier said to his friends: " Don't you think it's absurd that a Moroccan Berber youngster wanted to deceive an old Arab leader from Irak. By God Almighty, I'm able to send him an army that'll destroy him and his army overnight." Then he advised the caliphate to send him an army of the bedouins of Upper Egypt.

In the meantime, the Shi'its living in Ifrikya felt that they were neglected. Besides, they became aware that they were the main cause of all the disturbances and division between brothers and cousins. This dispersal policy was sown by the Shia sects to create an atmosphere of mutiny and uprisings in the country. Owing to this dismal situation, Moez Bin Badis endeavored to restore to normal the relationship between people of different sects and to reconcile between them. He also veered to the creed which most Ifrikyan people believed in, that is the Sunna creed. Thus he gained the sympathy of most people, especially in Kairwan whose inhabitants were mostly Sunnits. When he made a visit to Kairwan, his convoy was received heartily, and people cheered: "long live Al Moez!"

**As for the domestic policy the Sanhaji princes pursued, it turned sometimes to weakness and surrender. And like the Ubaidi princes, the Sanhaji princes indulged in likened to the Ubaidia's policy when they first governed Ifrikya; that is, it was either so strict that it became harsh and dictatorial, or excessively tolerant spending lavishly and liberally. They also donated so many gifts, and held plenty of**

**sumptuous banquets on religious occasions in such a way that they disposed of the greatest share of the country's fortune. As for the rabble, they were left the table left overs.**

The historian Ibnu Dinar narrated in his book, "The Close Friend" (Al Moenis) that when Al Moez's grandmother died in 411, he had made her coffin of very expensive wood (Indian wood), gem-studded, nailed with gold plates and adorned with luxurious jewelled necklaces. After burying her in Mahdia, he ordered fifty she-camels, one hundred oxen and one thousand sheep to be slaughtered and distributed on the rabble, in addition to thousands of dinars donated to them.

As for Youssef Balkin, the Berber prince, he enjoyed a luxurious life as Moez, the Arab prince did. He had four hundred female slave dancers in his palaces. It was told that his wives gave birth to seventeen baby boys in one day.

As a matter of fact, the extravagant life that the Ifrikyan princes used to live was due to the economic boom that Ifrikya haf known in those days, let not speak of the flourishing industry and the abundance of agriculture. The bedouin tribes also took part in that developing prosperity by being overtaxed. However, in spite of the princes' extravangancy, the historian Ibnul Athir told us that the Ifrikyan people were afflicted by an excessive inflation so that everything became very expensive. Turkish baths and bakeries sometimes closed. People began to starve. The rich people's wealth ran out, and epidemics became so widespread that in one day, between 500 and 700 people perished. Addabbegh, a scholar and historian, noted that many people immigratd to Sicily because life was easier, more secure, and the princes ruling there were more just and more righteous than their Ifrikyan counterparts.

By and large, on account of the miserable life that Ifrikya suffered, society became corrupt, and people lost their dignity. They became slavish, adulators and hypocritical. Moral degradation became the norm. Grades and high positions were not attained through competence, seriousness and assiduity, but through mediation, fame and power. So whoever reached a high position became more submissive and more servile to his boss rather than self-confident and respectful.

Ibnu Rashik's book, "The Mayor" ( Al Omda) brought out the increase of class segregation among the Ifrikyan people. He alluded often to the wide gap separating kings and upper-class people from the masses and the riff- raff. This shows that the Arab society was infected at that time by the disease of class division, extravagance, faked dignity and selfishness.

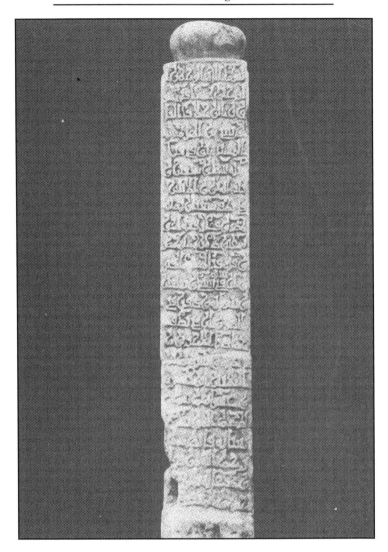

The gravestone of a dead man whose corpse was transported from Egypt to Kairwan. On the tomb was engraved the following:

"In the name of God the Gracious, the Merciful, this is the tomb of the late Abdoun Ibnu Jallad Annouassi, born in the town of Messila, Egypt. Died in 373, on Monday in the middle of Shabaan, (the eighth month just before the month of Ramadan). His brother brought his remains from Egypt and buried them in Kairwan graveyard in 376."

## IV.The Sanhaji vestiges:

Compared to the Aghlabites, the Sanhaji governors left only a few landmarks, because they thought that there was no need to erect more than what had been built or erected by their predecessors, the Aghlabites or the Ubaidi state. They implemented, brought to completion towers, forts, market places, Turkish baths and mosques. The Sanhajis were more inclined to suppress rebellions and fighting dissidents, in addition to their settlement not only in one capital city, but they were often on the move. They confined themselves to widen the existing establishments and institutions; they also cared about their renovations or their embellishment. If we exclude what Al Moez had built in Sabra, Kairwan, like palaces and market places that were entirely wiped out during the Hilalis' devastations, and if we also exclude what Al Moez had built for his aunt, Oum Milal, in Monastir (south east), and which was wiped out, too, like her palace or the mosque that carried the name of "The Lady" (Assaida), and which still stands erect, the Sanhaji princes did not leave any landmark in Tunisia more than what had already existed since the Aghlabites' or the Ubaidis'. They only completed what already been erected. They also made renovations of old mosques, like Moez's widening of the prayer hall of the Soussa Big Mosque, the renovation of its old pulpit dome and the minaret on the side of the mosque rampart. Besides, the Sanhaji prince, Al Mansur ordered the building of the prayer hall dome in Zeituna Mosque in Tunis. The Sanhaji princes were also interested in the decorating art, especially the artistic adornment they made for the wooden work of Okhba Mosque in Kairwan. Professor Suleimen Mustapha Zebbis, a modern Egyptian historian and archeologist pointed out that the decorating craftesmanship of the Sanhaji artists was unparalleled in the Moslem world.

**V.The scholastic activity:**

The scholastic activity in the Sanhaji era was an extension of the scholastic activities that had preceded it since the Islamic conquest. But life developed so rapidly in that era that attractions diversified, and the gap separating the social classes widened. Life became so paradoxical that confusing and inconsistant ideas prevailed over reason and logic, which led up to distrust and the lack of confidence between the people and the government on the one hand, and between the people themselves. For example, the close relationship that used to exist between the scholars and the laity almost disappeared. The laymen no longer supported the scholars in time of distress as the predecessors had done. Neither did they obey or compete to gain their sympathy or favor. Al Moez Ibnu Badis entered into intimate relation with the Sunnit scholar Mohamed Ibnu Abdessamad, then he schemed to assassinate him. His supporters first stood on his side and revolted against the prince. But when they saw that their fate was at stake, they did not only withdraw, but they turned against the poor scholar and started disparaging him. Besides, the Ifrikyan laymen lost their veracity and behaved cowardly and hypocritically. The same could be said of the scholars and learned men. They did their best to have close relations with the prince and the men of power although in their inner selves, they despised them.They also led a paradoxical life unprincipled and full of contradictions.

The poet Ibnu Rashik mentioned the example of Imam Atick Mohamed Ibnu Bakr Al Warrak. Ibnu Rashik went one day to Okhba Mosque; he found Sheikh Warrak sat in a circle of students reading to them some Islamic precepts and alludung in his lecture to some previous jurist. While reading, tears streamed down his face out of grief and regret for the loss of the olden times. In the evening, Ibnu Rashik went to Warrak's home. He astonishingly found him in a circle of friends laughing and cracking jokes.

He addressed the Imam in a tone of reproach: You shiekh, how different this lifestyle you're leading is from the lifestyle I witnessed in the mosque!" Al Warrak replied: "In the first circle you saw me, I'm in God's abode. But now I'm at home. I can do whatever pleases me."

Those people lived two sorts of life, the life of faked appearances in which they pretended to be pious, God-fearing and humility, and the second was their truthful way of life.

However, there remained a few scholars who were honest, principled and loyal to their creed. Ibnu Rashik gave the example of other scholars who remained Godly, confident in their belief and sticking to the way of life they chose for themselves, like Abul Hassan Al Gaboussi, Abu Omran Al Fessi, Abul Kassem Allabidi and others whom people trusted their knowledge and their theological works. However, the Sanhaji princes apparantly complied with the public's opinion and attitude, but they intrinsically conformed to the Shi'its'scholars'opinion despite their being unconvinced by its pertinence and logic.To be clearer, they appeared to be in favor of the majority of people who were Sunnits, but in truth, they were in favor of the Shi'its' minority. Prince Al Moez showed publicly to be siding with the Sunnit scholars, but he was not indeed. This is the case of a Shi'it Imam called Abu Issaac who was judged publicly to be a miscreant when he declared that Ali was the most intimate companion of Prophet Mohamed (PUB). So the public wanted him to withdraw what he said on the pulpit of Okhba Mosque on Friday prayer or he would be punished, but he refused and the prince did not punish him. Besides, when he died, the prince attended his funerals and made them pompous.

All these examples showed how the people, the authorities and the scholars were no longer as their predecessors were, honest, sincere, truly pious and self-confident.

## VI. Some Sunnit scholars in the Sanhaji era:

### 1. Abul Hassan Al Kaboussi:

Aboul Hassan was not from Gabes (south east of Tunisia) as his name suggested, but he was nicknamed so because his uncle used to wear his turban tight on his head as the people of Gabes did.

Abul Hassan first studied in Ifrikya, then he went to Mecca on pilgrimage. He acquired knowledge from famous scholars in Mecca and in Egypt, too. When he returned to Kairwan, many students learned from him. He was a great narrator versed in Hadith and jurisprudence. Among his works one can mention, "Introduction to Jurisprudence", "A book for Instructors and Learners", "Trust in God".

Abul Hassan died in Kairwan in 403 and was buried in Kairwan's Hattabia graveyard. Although he was blind, he was very accurate in his judgment.

Abu Bakr Al Maliki, a scholar, described Abul Hassan as, "a pious, God-fearing, truthful and honest when giving sermons. People attended his circle of learning in great number. He became beloved and venerated, and gained such a great popularity that the Sultan sent him a forewarning. It was narrated that when he died, a hundred poets continued to eligize him for a whole year after his death.

### 2. Abou Omran Al fessi:

He learned from Abul Hassan first, then immigrated to kordoba in Andalusia and to the Middle East to pursue his studies. When he returned to Kairwan, he taught the Holy Koran , jurisprudence and narrated the Prophet's Hadith. Whenever he made a lecture, it was literally recorded. He died in 430 and people frequently visited his tomb to read Al Fatiha. (the first sura or chapter in the Koran)

Apart from scholars and theologians, Kairwan knew learned men in other fields of knowledge, like mathematicians, physicists and physicians.

### 3. Abdelmomen Al Kindi:

He was distinguished as a mathematician.

### 4. Ahmed Ibnul Jazzar:

He was known as a physician. He became versed in medicine. He devoted himself to the treatment of sick people. He wrote a book in the treatment of diseases entitled, "Provisions for the traveler" (Zed Al Mousafer). He wrote another book dealing with the description of drugs called, "The Best Resort" (Al Aatimad).European scientists of the Middle Ages translated many of his books into Latin.Besides his books on medicine, Ibnul Jazzar wrote books in history, like "The Definition of True History", and another book entitled, "Information about the state". Ibnul Jazzar died in Kairwan at the age of eighty in 369.

A poet called Kashejim wrote a panegyric lauding him. The poem goes as follows:

"Abu Jaafar, I saw throngs of learned men and wizards rushing upon your book, 'Provisions for the Traveler'. I became convinced that had John, Christ's apostle, been still alive, he would have obviously call your book perfection. I would commend Ahmed (Abu Jaafar's first name) for the good services that he achieved,

Whose traces are still apparent on noble-minded people who are grateful to the one known for his good-heartedness and generosity."

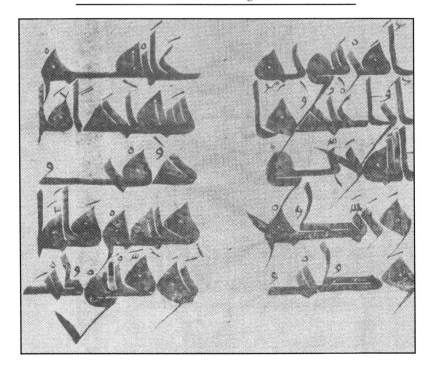

*A page of the Holy Koran Kufic-written on a piece of parchment and posted on the door of the Big Moque by Fatima, Al Moez's nursemaid. On this parchment was written a verse of the Holy Koran which reads: "You Ordained me (Prophet Mohamed addressing God) that they should (his people in Mecca) worship only God, my God and theirs, and Thou art their Witness for Eternity."*

## VII. The literary movement:

The Sanhaji era was distinguished by its fine arts and literature. It was the golden age in Kairwan and Ifrikya, particularly during the reign of Al Moez Bin Badis. This is due to the population increase, the abundance of prosperity, the presence of stability, the development of welfare, culture and the emergence of a refined civilization.

However, those positive factors were not the outcome of an era, but the outcome of the previous succeeding eras, the fruit of many experiences, and the the essence of various civilizations. It was also when multidinous cultures of different eastern civilizations, like Egyptian, Irakyan, Syrian and Andalusian that had a resounding echo on Ifrikyan towns, particularly Kairwan.

Many middle eastern men of culture and literature used to visit the literary circles and salons in Ifrikya and particularly in Kairwan, like Nathr Ibnul Abid, Badii Ezzamen Al Hamadhani, Al Moutanabbi, Al Maarri, Abi Hayan Attauhidi and other numberless thinkers and poets.

Abu Ali Ibnu Rabii sent a letter to Mghira Ibnu Hazm in the Middle East describing the rapid propagation of the news in that age. He wrote:

"Nothing separates you from us but a short distance that we have to cross on horseback, camel back or a short distance by boat. If any of the latest news spreads out in your country, it is heard by our dead in their tombs and by the living in their houses and their palaces."

What also contributed to the development of culture and the literary movement in Ifrikya was the abundant prosperity and the luxurious idleness that Al Moez Ibnu Badis entertained so much so that he ordered the doors of his palace to be wide open for hundreds of poets and literary men, bestowing on them thousands of dinars, and allowing them to hold competitive poetic circles where they recited all sorts of lyric and panegyric poems.

Ahmed Amin, a modern Egyptian writer and novelist commented upon that era for its thriving poetry wrote: " Because its main subjects were based on eulogy, Arab poetry would not flourish so widely and so rapidly if kings' and princes' palaces were not open for poets to entertain those men of power and laud their achievements and their generosity."

Many poets became more prominent than others because their poems were appraised by princes and rich people.

## 1. Ibnu Rashik:

He was the most renouned poet in Ifrikya at that time. His full name is Abdullah Al Hassan Ibnu Rashik. He was born in Mhammadia (the southern suburbs of Tunis) in 390. He left for Kairwan in his teens and studied literature and literary criticism under the great grammarian Abi Abdullah Al Gazzaz. He associated with Kairwan's poets like Ali Ibnu Abi Arrajel, Abdel Karim Innahjali, Mohamed Ibnu Sharaf and others.

Ibnu Rashik was such a prestigious poet and writer that Al Moez made him his bosom friend and companion. He wrote many panegyric poems lauding that prince.

Ibnu Rashik stayed in Kairwan until the Hilalyin tribes assailed that city and devastated it. Then he moved to Sicily and stayed there until his death in 456.

These are excerpts of his laudatory poems in which he praised Al Moez:

"When you alighted on the mounts of Sabra and made it your abode, Sabra welcomed you so generously, you man of generosity and honor. Its buildings extended widely and embraced the most valuable sweet-smelling gardens of wild flowers. Then man of magnificence, you started subjugating bravely those vile people who alighted downhill at Ghimdan." (It may be the name of a town or a place)

Ibnu Rashik had many entertaining companions, like his bosom friend the poet Ibnu Sharaf. They often met to tell anecdotes and satirical poems.

In this excerpt of a poem in which Ibnu Sharaf asked him to write in favor of Andalusia and not against it. Ibnu Rashik wrote:

"What I found humiliating in the land of Andalusia those who claimed to be qualified and powerful. Irrelevant surnames given to a venerable kingdom sounds like a cat boasting the power of a lion."

Ibnu Sharaf replied him criticizingly:

"If exile has cast you amongst people whom you deem to be hateful, you have to condescend as long as you are staying in their land and in their home."

In addition to his being an unparalleled poet, Ibnu Rashik studied deeply literature and literary criticism. He became versed in the history of the Arabs, their eloquence in poetry and their elaborately written prose. This can be seen in his book, "The Pillar". In this book, he dealt with the writing of poetry, its strength and its shortcomings.

Ibnu Khaldun, the Tunisian historian and sociologist commented upon Ibnu Rashik's book. He wrote: " this book is unequalled in handling the subject of poetry. None has ever written better than Ibnu Rashik about this subject."

Ibnu Rashik's style of criticism is distinguished by its meticulous analysis of the form and content of a text or a poem, his thorough study of its different aspects in a clear and elaborate style. His approach is deductive, it starts with the general and goes to the detail. As for his poetry, it is marked by the use of articulated and expressive words and a lucid uncomplicated form, reitarating what other poets had written before him. So his poetry had nothing particular or distinctive, but it is beautifully and clearly expressed. It dealt with many subjects very common in his time, like elegies, erotic and descriptive poetry.

In this poem, Ibnu Rashik dealt with the means of subsistence which were unusual, when not based on something firm and steadfast, but ephemeral earned from perverted means. He said, probably satirizing these easy ways;

"The child earns his livelihood not by labor or by the sweat of his brow, but through easy means. If any livelihood is attained without hard work, God's hope in earning it in an easy way is the only means of attaining it."

As for Ibnu Rashik's prose, it was written in a beautiful, clear and comprehensible style. In fact, Ibnu Rashik was as fluent and smooth in writing as in speaking. This is a thesis he wrote about traveling:

"The example of a man with a sendentary life-style is like stagnant water. If left, it changes. But when it moves, it becomes turbid. However, the example of a traveler is like a rainy cloud. There are those who invoke it for mercy, and those who impricate it as if it were a sign of wrath."

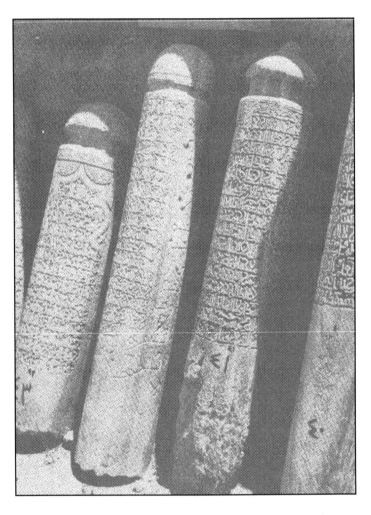

*Tombs which date back to the Sanhaji era. Found
in Kouraishi's graveyard in Kairwan.*

**2.Ibnu Sharaf:**

his full name is Abdullah Mohamed Ibnu Sharaf. His grandfather came to Kairwan from the Arabian peninsula during the conquest of Ifrikya. He was born in Kairwan and he grew up in quest of religious and literary study when Kairwan was in the climax of flourishing knowledge and science. He studied under Abil Hassan Al Kaboussi and Abi Omran Al Farissi. He contributed with his rich writings and poems to the development of the literary circles of the time. He was both a gifted writer and poet.

When disturbances increased in Kairwan, he moved to Mahdia and came into contact with prince Al Moez and his son Tamim. After that, he went to Sicily and acquainted with its prince. Finally, he immigrated to Andalusia and travelled round its towns until he died in Sevil in 460.

His best writings in literary criticism is "A Treatise about the Renouned Scholars in Islamic Philosophy". In this book, he dealt with Arab poets and poetry. He surveyed the evolution of poetry from Pre-Islamic time to the age he lived in. He dealt with each poet apart, his biography, his features and his poems.

He wrote about Ibou Nouas, an Iraki wine poet the following criticism:

"Abou Nouas was the first to breach with the norms of poetry. He deviated from all that is righteous, turning seriousness into ridicule, the difficult into facile. He loosened what is stressed and put into confusion what is ordered. (Ibnu sharaf alluded to what is grammatically construed in the Arabic language). Things became incomprehensible in Abu Nouas's poetry and its eloquence, which degraded Arabic poetry at that time and made it lose its value and its glamor. But in spite of all these defects, people were fond of Abou Nouas's poetry. His poetry was sold at high prices in markets and readers exchanged his poems.Unfortunately,they were fond of what is ridiculous and weak and prefered it to what is serious and significant."

We can deduce from these comments that although Ibnu Sharaf was a poet and a literary man, he rejected not only what is immoral and irreligious in poetry,but also what is stylistically insipid and poor; this is due to the fact that religion, moral values and refined had still such a great impact on poets and writers of Kairwan at that time.

Ibnu Sharf's poetry is elaborately expressive and skillfully imaginative. In this poem, he described the disastrous condition of his children after the calamity that befell Kairwan. He wrote:

"My children and myself look like pigeons strayed away from their nests at night. We know no sleep and feel restless and fidgety. It is as if my children did not enjoy any comfort or bounty that had delighted their lives in Kairwan's heyday."

In another poem, he deplored Kairwan and cried over a lost happy past. He said:

"Kairwan, I wish I were a bird surveying and contemplate deeply your past like a thinker and a researcher.The remembrance of your benefactions did not let me forget my grief. Would my sickness disappear through any expediency. Had I known that their end (the people of Kairwan) had come along with my departure, I would have done what I did not do."

Ibnu Sharaf wrote in prose a beautiful thesis about a blind poet called Bashar Ibnu Bourd.

"Bashar's poetry can be considered at the forefront of modernization although he lived through two eras. He lived in the last days of the Ubaidi era and the early Sanhaji era. He was fond of listenting to poetry. His poetry was comprehensive. It dealt with women's love, men's bravery and other multidinous subjects. He was so lenient that he became sometimes too affectionate, and at other time so powerful that he became too haughty. He lived so long that he wrote so profusely; his poetry overflowed like the sea and his fame spread all over the Arab world."

### 3. Abul Hassan Al Houssari:

He was Abi Isaak Ibrahim Al Houssari's cousin. He was renouned for his book, "The Flower of Literary Works". Abul Hassan was born in Kairwan in 420 in a family whose ancestors were the grandchildren of Okhba Ibnu Nafaa Al Fehri.

He learned the Holy Koran and studied the art of the Koran's recitation. He also studied theology, Arabic and the arts of poetry and prose. He lost his eyesight since he was a child, but this loss was compensated by a discerning insight, an extrasensory perception and pertinent thinking. Talking about his blindness, he wrote:

"People say I am blind, but I am more sightful than those endowed with eyesight. The darkness of my sight made my heart darker, and both endowed me with good insight into the nature of things."

As for his doctrine, Al Houssari was a devoted Sunnit who repudiated the Shia doctrine. This idea confirmed what he wrote in the introduction of his poetic works:

"Keep away from what happened between them (the Shi'its). God's Justice was done because of their misdeeds. Will God forgive them. Only God Knew their true intention and their inward thoughts."

When Kairwan was afflicted with the disastrous fall through the Shiaa disturbances and the devastation of the Hilali tribes, Al Houssari moved to Andalusia. His poetry helped him gain a favored position among the sectarian kings, particularly with Moutamad Bin Abbed, the king of Sevil whom Al Houssari lauded extravagantly in his praising poems.

Although Al Houssari was hospitably entertained in Andalusia, he never forgot the calamitous devastation that befell Kairwan. He wrote in one of his poems the love and pity that he felt for the people of Kairwan:

"My beloved people, never did I fail to keep my promise to you, nor did I fail to keep my warm-hearted affection for you. However distant you are from me and the sea separates us, our souls will visit each other during sleep. I won't sleep but to visit your sprits. How can I, living in asylum, feel comfort and quietude in my sleep?"

Trying to find excuses for having emigrated from his home, he said:

"Hadn't been those carrying winds, I wouldn't have mounted this dark green horse and that squinting-eyed horse. Living in one's country in poverty is much more favorable than home-sickness in prosperity."

Al Houssari excelled in poetry and he enthralled those who read his poems. Ibnu Bassem, one of those who were infatuated by Al Houssari's poetry wrote in his book, "The Holy Relic":

"Al Houssari was a flowing ocean and a manufacturing mind of poetry. He was a leading poet. He immigrated to Andalusia in the mid five hundred year of the Hejir after the devastation of Kairwan when literature and poetry were in their climax. He became the cynosure of the sectarian kings in Andalusia who competed in order to have Al Houssari in their palaces, like those who compete to settle in the abode of eternal bliss."

Among the most illustrious poems of Al Houssari, and which many poets, east and west tried to emulate but to no avail is this poem in which he sang his imaginative lover:

"How long will the night of lovers last? Will Doomsday be its appointed time?...

By God, endow the lover with some sleep, your vision (the beloved female) will bring him full bliss.

He suffers from sleeplessness, and the stars grieve for his sorrowful condition.

He is infatuated with the beauty of his slender sweetheart fearing the spiers to denounce him to those who are jealous of him.

I feel sleepless all night, and my eyes are aching with fatigue,

trying to catch sight of my lover whose charming beauty, like astatue, fascinates me without worshipping her.

I am a martyr of love, but my sweetheart did not respond to my torments.

Her sadness for my condition is apparent on her cheeks, I wonder why your eyes disavows it.

Your fascinating love is killing, but I doubt that it is deliberate.

By God, I plead you, let your apparition fill me with bliss so that your longing lover enjoy some sleep."

It goes without saying that the original text is more beautifully written and more eloquent than the paraphrased translation of it. Nevertheless, I tried to include the main ideas of the poems. It is to be noted that Al Houssari was blind, but the expressions that he used in describing the fascinating beauty of his sweetheart is very telling. Besides, Al Houssari was a zealous Sunnit, and however beautiful was his fictional beloved one, he would never use use the term 'worship' to describe for his excessive love for his lover. He used words like 'fascinate, infatuate' but he would use the word 'worship' when he alluded to God because Islam states that none is worshipped but God.

*A general view of the immortal city of Kairwan.*

# The translator's biography

Negra Mohamed Fadhel (born,1944) is aretired English teacher. He taught English in high schools in Kairwan (1973-1978), the he was nominated assistant professor in the Arts Faculty in Kairwan and worked there for ten years (1985- mid 1996). Between 1978-1984, he was appointed vice-principal, then principal in high schools in Kassrine (centre west) and in kairwan. From 1996 to 2006 he taught English in Riyadh, Saudi Arabia in King Fahad Security College (1996-2000), then Riyadh Technical College (2001-2006). He also taught English in language schools both in Tunisia and in Saudi Arabia (1979-2004).

Mr. Mohamed Fadhel is a write and translator. He translated Tunisian folktales written by the late Tunisian story teller and radio announcer, Abddel Aziz Al Aroui. Four of the 33 translated foltales were published in an American folktale journal called 'Tale Trader'(1993-1999). These folktales are still waiting to be published. The translator's wish is that one publishing house would be willing to edit and publish them.

Mr. Mohamed Fadhel wrote a texbook for EFL students containing 32 world wide short stories accompanied by comrehension questions, grammar and vocabulary exercises, short poems, puzzles and jokes for fun. The textbook is entitled "A Textbook For Extensive Reading". The book is not published yet and is waiting to be published.

The second translated book is "Kairwan Through The Ages", that is the existing book and is waiting to be published. Mr. Mohamed Fadhel translated this book, written by his brother, Dr. Touhami Negra. The book is translated in comemoration of the illustrious year, (2009,1430) decreed by president Zine Al Abidin as the year of "Kairwan, the capital of Islamic Culture".